SavageSzn

By

Faythe Ayanna Missick

Please direct all inquiries to Missick Publishing Co., LLC

Missick Publishing Company, LLC/ Missickpublishingco@gmail.com

Savage Szn Logo: Robbie Wilburn

Book Cover Designed by: Myles Grio

Copyright ©. 2018. Faythe Missick

ISBN13: 978-1987728651/ ISBN10: 1987728653

Printed in the United States of America.

SAVAGESZN

Savage. Seen to many as someone who is - reckless, uncontrolled, and uncivilized, in the eyes of society. Savage. Exactly what I strive to be; on my own terms. I choose not to let society define me or pick my choices. I choose to be fierce and violent towards my enemies - killing negativity that may try to cause me to fail. This doesn't particularly mean my life was "shitty", it just wasn't satisfying. I was making my own decisions but I wasn't aggressive enough. So, I sped up my process, amplified my approach. With some help from God... I "upgraded" my life. I had enough faith in my belief in knowing I did not have to live the way I was living. And so I faithfully believed that I could not walk into this action. Oh no - I needed to take any and all means necessary and aggressively put myself into the position I wanted to be in. Savage

Savage Szn: "Living the life as a woman and managing your sanity"

THE INTRO

I found myself diving back into my past through my pictures/videos to do a memory blast for my snap followers. What a time I had during Savage Szn! The highlight of this action oriented season lands between August and October - because it looked like my friends and I were living our... "BEST" lives! The bottles were... poppin, the hookahs were... smoking, our faces were beat and waist snatched! I was coming down off my "thick era" so my booty-waist ratio was in my favor!

People constantly question, "What is Savage Szn?". My female friends, define this era as: every time a f*** nigga does something, that calls out the age-old "statement". While male counterparts view it as a way for girls to embrace their "thotness". The word "savage" is so common nowadays, I find it hard to define it at times. So the question remains wildly open to interpretation.

But it is just that, savage szn. I mean, I know I am grammatically incorrect with answering a question with a question. But - I cannot explain what is unspoken. A good friend has always said, "What's understood doesn't need to be explained." Personally, I never thought I would EVER have to actually explain it because it was not for everyone else, it was my journey. It so happened that people *wanted* to be apart of it. My friends wanted to liberate me in this movement and people that were watching from near and far, wanted to figure out exactly what the title I gave this era was. Savage Szn, would definitely be categorized as individualism. Because my idea of individuality also includes people combined with the extrovert in me, it grew to be something social. Even with it being social it does not take a way from what it does for me, did for me and will do for me.

Let's back track to 25. It is hard being 25. Although, the one age that I think may be worse than 25 is being 26 because you are one step closer to 30. You are one step closer to the pressures of being in a career, being in a relationship, being out of your mother's house and of course being independent. 30, the age of NO return! Y'all don't even understand the struggle of holding onto NOT getting off my parents' phone plan. I have been holding on with all my strength and graces because I KNOW that's the final step into adulthood. Birthdays - just not much of a celebration anymore, its shaped up to give space to reflect on the amount of time you have to get your shit together. In my reflection, I can't believe I made it through a time where things would and were projected to crumble into order. Beautifully, savagely, year 25 unfolded into something that would give me peace and satisfaction.

So now, is it the partying that allows me to cope with the things life throws at me? I can't lie, old college days bring reminiscence of drinking Bacardi 151 like it was juice. Talk about Savage!

College. Freshman year - one of the worst years for my family. Our finances were shitty, our health was shitty, and my grades were shitty. When my university told me I couldn't come back the next semester, I had the platform to aggressively take action and fight it. Let me paint this picture: not only did I have a 1.67 GPA, I also didn't even have the money to pay them to get back in. God said have a seat and so I did, looking around and looking back, he meant it. With the amount of alcohol that was being consumed, my mind was taking a toll on me as well. With that definition of "Savage" which then I thought was just doing whatever I wanted to do, did not have a clear vision or even a purpose. The Savage in me then, can't even compare to who that experience created now. I didn't care about life and wasn't in a place where I could see the end, because *everything* was screwed up, anyway. That screwed up aimlessness is not what my current Savage Szn embodies. For me, Savage Szn manifested when I didn't even expect it to. Once I created a vision for where I wanted to be, how I wanted to get there, and when I wanted to get there, that's when I could show up and show out; I really just allowed God to show me what he was going to do in the first place. But this only came when he saw I was ready for the transformation.

I eventually declared a sense of "Savagery" over my life. I swear you are not officially living Savage life unless you are saying 50 million times to yourself, over your social media, and taking shots to Savage Szn every time you are out. Well, at least that's how I was putting the message out there. This transformation season kicked off when I noticed a shift in my lifestyle, followed by me wanting to let people know that although I was going through it, I was okay. This led to me thinking people liked the movement and they should be able to live by some of the same values I stand by. With Savage Szn being my individual way of coping, it was people who made me realize it was more than just mourning. I found myself continuously explaining what it is and what was manifesting.

It was a change in my lifestyle. They say something like, words are in the power of the tongue. I can attest to that in my Prayer List. Everything I prayed for became my reality, speaking it into existence or just saying it enough that I began to live a lifestyle that brought me changes. I watched everything on that list get crossed out, week after week...action after action. I believe it was the idea that I was able to have enough faith that I could tell God exactly what I wanted, and trust that he would give me everything I asked for. Understanding we all have customized relationships with our guiding power or divinity, those who can't relate to the same God I hold on to, I still believe there should be a higher power/values that are the light of your daily life.

It's similar to when people say if you lie enough you will began to believe that lie. Yea, based on my reflection of my season of savage manifestation, I think it is the same for when you speak things into existence. I do believe speaking up things into your life, you change the way you move and your actions become what you speak them up to be. Another bible quote, "faith without works..." confirms that the faith has to coupled and married to action. {Most of you know my father is a Pastor, so don't throw the bible at me because I quoted something wrong. IF that's what you're worried about - you're not reading for the right reasons. IF that's the case… oh well, because I already got your coins from the purchase. THANKS!}

In the same breath, Savage Szn, denounces the idea of caring. Not in losing care for yourself, but the idea of caring for things. Things, people and situations that hold you back from caring about your most prized possession; yourself. It challenges the savage-in-training to use your energy for caring about what you *want* to do. It challenges what your expectations in life are for yourself. I believed in eliminating the distractions and the toxicity even when I didn't initially realize they were distractions. The seasons that end when you phase into another one are exhilarating in experience. Savage Szn is the season of taking full control of what I want in life and that is exhilaratingly powerful. Again, not taking away from God's plan but putting your full potential into full effect and taking responsibility for the things that happen in your life. I am fully aware of everything that sucks, did suck and may potentially suck in my life and I take responsibility for my feelings. When I am feeling cemented in those feelings, I allow myself to be, to deal with it and then channel energy to grow from it.

Positivity seems to be a leading drive to being this "Savage". Even with positivity, the negative is what drives you to that place of aggressively pushing further. It's a delicate balance of yin and yang. Whether that negativity comes from outside or within, you cannot know what it means to channel positive vibes if you have never lived the negative. I aim to be self aware and honest in recognizing my mistakes. I also stand very aware of when I am in a state of being content. I am content in the idea that I am not perfect; that there will be many days that I do not want to fight and 25 taught me that is ok. But if I keep my mind on the idea of where I have put myself in my future, in my head already, I cannot focus on anything else but being a Savage.

I need *everything* by *any* means necessary. I get what I need by *any* means necessary. I have aligned my priorities in a way that allow me to be a Savage because I, Faythe, said so.

25 taught me that I'll know I've found the "one" when he loves me as much as I love myself. The misconception is that Savage Szn kicks in when you're single or post catastrophic break-up but it's so much more than that. Another trip down memory lane - one of my friends called me as soon as she got played in what we can now call a situationship. Finding herself back at square one of finding the "one" and shy of being in a relationship, the guy was extremely disrespectful of the woman that she was and had become. Me, not the sensitive friend because I just never have the words to say...suggested we go out. {*This happened to fall on the same night my aunt passed and we got pretty intoxicated. So as a warning, if you not tryna grab a bottle, I am not the friend to call for the aforementioned catastrophe, especially when I'm navigating loss ...*} She immediately thought she got the 30-day trial Savage Szn subscription. To which I told her you can't join when you're still crying. You are not in a position to even fathom the experience, the full effect of this phenomena or the growth that comes from this season. As a rule of membership, you have to begin by becoming aligned with your end goal.

I do subscribe to what y'all call meditation, not even knowing that's what it was. I grew up in church and we call it worship. To put peace in my mind, I pause the marathon of thoughts and focus on God, then me. Can you take a few minutes to not think about anyone else in the world and truly focus on yourself? It's so hard because we constantly have a million things simultaneously going through our minds. For me, it is just easier to focus on God and through focusing on him, I can reflect on my life.

"God give me peace and direction." is my mantra. My meditative song of reason.

8

Savage Szn is an ongoing process of dealing with yourself. I want to acknowledge the idea of being able to deal with myself. I cannot be anything other than me, so I might as well be the best me that I can be. Who is to label and dictate what the right aspect of making one happy is limited to?

Be careful what you want as happiness. It may be a cost to some non-related areas in life that you thought were where you wanted to be. More often than never, it wasn't where you were supposed to remain.

So what am I doing through these pages of words, testimony and experiences? I'm for sure am not giving you steps on *how* to live your life. Rather I'm hoping you can relate to my own experiences - you have to live for you! You have to practice individualism and not group yourself into a category that starts defining you and directing you to do what everyone else does. Let your higher power guide you into achieving your goals without taking no for an answer. Take action, never take "no".

ADAPTATION

In life, we are presented with a series of situations that may often conflict. Based on the decisions we make, our lives can either be satisfying or miserable - I choose to live in positivity. I choose to create my own opportunities that lead me to success. I choose to love God and put him first in everything that I do.

You have to make the right choices in life for you regardless of your situation.

This idea of ...choices.

I do think however, we should be grateful for options and the experiences that present themselves on our paths. When you start reflecting about how life is unfolding before you, possibly how "messed up" your life is - think about the fact that you don't have to stay in one lane. Some people don't acknowledge they've being doing 60mph in the same lane and in the same direction. They believe their situation chooses the way they live and for this neglect of choice, they're ultimately living in their limitations.

Exhibit A: You complain everyday about your weight. Maybe not verbally expressing it but it fucks with your head. When you're trying things on, when your friends make suggestions... you automatically get defensive. You HAVE the option to have a body that you are content with. I hate being a sample size. Specifically, because I had one year of being the thick friend and then just like that I lost my butt and some self-esteem. I will not wear dresses - I think they are not flattering on me because I look like I am going to fall over. Pants are my best friend - but this is a choice. I would rather not do squats every day because I want to be lazy and gain weight. So, my get fit plan looks like me wanting to eat pasta and Popeyes every day. But realistically, I can't get an accurate result because I don't want the option that is going to do the work. It's not a priority, I don't recognize it or even put it on my list of things that will make me feel better. Lazy, eh lol.

It's the idea of adapting to a situation, altering your life to fit your circumstances. You choose to play the cards you have been dealt and when to walk away from the game. My life gave me what it gave me and I chose to keep playing, until I was playing the cards I *wanted* to play.

I choose to believe that everything happens for a reason and the idea of faith is what makes us strong when we have to be vulnerable.

You are the only one that can tap into the choices that have been presented before you. The craziest part of your experience with this book is that you already know everything I will lay out and still not tap into aggressively generating your own season. Accountability is another great element and it humbles that inner you, the quiet parts of your mind. My Pastor, on one Sunday talked about God speaking to Simon and giving him a new name. Although he gave him a new name that would define his new purpose and missions in life, the old Simon, would tend to appear when things got rough.

I decided to give myself a new name when I named myself Savage. I didn't do any voodoo or nonsense, I didn't fill the air with pounds of sage smoke and meditative candles. My new name, symbolized the way I would change my lifestyle. A lifestyle that was tired of living the way I was living.

My mom and sister shared their individual prayer lists and so I sat down one day and generated my own. I knew I could make better and more progressive decisions with the guidance of a higher power and faith on my shoulders. So I started with #1 and faithfully listed my prayers.

You know, to this day, I still talk to people about *BlkGirlNChina* and the glory of traveling. People still approach me with finances being what's holding them back from taking that plane, train, bus, car, walk, etc. If my parents folded everytime they didn't have the money, I would have not been a college graduate. Sacrifices are a choice - you choose to live your life paying bills every month and not going anywhere. I chose to work two jobs so that I could create an experience. My visions and perceptions in life are certainly not better than anybody else's but I hang around people that are regarded as amazing people. Not because of what they have but because of the choices they have made. In times of abundance, in times of lack...in moments they didn't have all the means to the end...yet in their lives they've found a way and surpassed what they initially set out to do. With that, they are able to inspire me.

I've found that people still create their idea of happiness based on the people that they have in their lives, instead of being inspired by their actions and gains. When you're little you want to have friends - your cousins are your first friends and why does that matter? Because my boss told me that people want to matter to other people and he was absolutely right! He used the example of when you're on the playground and you're not picked for the kickball game. It sucks because not only do you think you can't play but because you think nobody likes you. Double hurt. We go on social media every day and post pics and statuses hoping that people will like it and that will validate the type of person you are or have presented for the crowd. "Are you a person that is mostly liked or mostly nah?" In terms of your own happiness why do you care? If I am living in my truth I am bound to piss a few people off because human beings can't stand to see someone looking happier than they are. My circle - we move the same way.

The moment you chose to figure out why you are all you need, on your journey to make yourself a better person... you are changing your lifestyle. You began to live with a new purpose that you didn't even think was an option.

25 was a great year! Well, it at least looked good to everyone else. What I presented and created, looked good! I wrote my first book, I had a great romantic relationship, I just moved into my new apartment, and I bought my first car. Wow, I had a lot to be thankful for.

It looked cute or wateva but let's just note, get this out of the way, that I was exhausted. I was working all day to make ends meet and not being appreciated by the work place I was dedicating my 9-5 to. I was working to keep my man happy, although I didn't see it as a job. I thought I was happy. In reflection, I was only motivated by how I was being perceived. Keeping up this image kept me driving in the direction I was going. Why the hell did I do that?! I had taken a few steps back from being a risk taker and became comfortable in my stress. I bought into the norm that says life is supposed to be stressful, it's life! If you're working hard enough, then you're living! Well, if I learned anything from long days with short nights, it's that if this is your life, you're not going to have it too long. Studies, articles and science have reported that stress will KILL you!

My prayer list not only helped me to trust in my happiness but it helped me define where I wanted to be as a person. I've listed what things made this list that helped me navigate Savage Szn:

- ✓ Closer to God- If I would have known that the situations that drew me nearer to God would be so traumatic, I would ask that he go back in time and do it <u>exactly</u> the way he did it.
- ✓ Financially Comfortable- I grew up in a household that lived paycheck to paycheck and that is not where I wanted to be. I need that comfortability where even if I don't have a savings, I am living at a comfortable level within my expenditures. May my wealth overflow, I called on God and said I need you to come in abundance.
- ✓ Career- I wanted somewhere that I could not only grow but where I could be appreciated. I've been in too many positions where my supervisor has criticized my intentions without any feedback. If you are a parent, how do you expect your child to grow if you don't give them suggestions on how. I don't need a job that will be my mother

but correct me when I am wrong. A place that will give me praise not just when I am right but when I have exceeded the expectation. Closer to my career goals in education: Pretty direct, because my mother told me to be specific. She challenged my original thought with, "Why are you praying for a job that you don't even really want and when he gives it to you, you're going to get fired because you didn't want the job you wanted the pay!" Thus, I got more specific, I wanted a better understanding of what my purpose in life is.

✓ Healthier- I didn't really want to be healthier I just wanted my stomach flat and my booty poking out more, manifestation lol. I'd just like to first and foremost thank GOD, then I would like to thank the angels of sculpting for giving me a body that may not be perfect for everybody but it's damn sure perfect for most! Amen

I chose to make a Prayer List and not only write it down but pray on it and watch how I speak my change in lifestyle into existence.

Little did I know this list would get deep and I would grow in appreciating who I am and what I live for!

Trust me, when I first started this list it was much longer. But as time went on I eliminated, combined and re-evaluated what was important in life.

Closer to God

I think we all need something that spiritually connects us with another world. A world outside of our fucked-up triage of realities we call work, family, and finances.

My spirit yearned for more - I wanted and will always yearn to be a more relatable representation of God. I want to be a good vibe so that it is understood that, that is all that is accepted in my proximity. I want my energy to be contagious enough that you can't help talking about me without mentioning the positive effect I put into the atmosphere. I cannot walk through the halls, speaking and greeting people who do not benefit my life without being an image of God. You can talk about what I have done but you can't forget who I am, in short I want my presence to leave an impact of joy and peace.

My places that I've come to call work have all had a contrasting yet reoccurring vibe that I've recognized. Everybody is always on 10, whether it's fueled by caffeine or passion or power, everyone operates with very high energy. Until adding educator on my resume with my current district, I thought the law firm was intense. Walking the halls right after an interim test... people are on edge and operating at that exaggerated 10. I have learned to keep calm and I would have not been able to do that if it was not for me being drawn to openness in my relationship with God.

This summer life was more fucked up than the imagined, cocktail in hand, wind in hair and summer sun beaming on my skin. Life was starting to question if I really wanted to be close to God. If so, how close? I had no choice but to be in the same seat sitting with him. Not next to but sitting in the same seat! I let go of things, not by choice or utilization of free will but because you should be careful in what you ask for.

I asked for more and so God gave me less.

TRAGIC

So this is what happened that was deemed as a tragedy. I never delete my experiences and as I write this, I must include a very minimal view to how this experience became a tragic tale. The foolishness, that went through my head when who we will refer to as "idiot" made quite the idiotic decision in his life that propelled me into square one of what I've outlined as Savagery. I have to let y'all read this because...Lord if this isn't the bitterest thing! {Chi Chi told me it was bitter and yet I still ignored her!!!!! Here we are. Lmao Chinenye - this is for you and the rest of my friends who would not let me expose/provide even this minimal shine in my product of empowerment.} I would be lying before God if I told you that this break up had nothing to do with Savage Szn. Hell, it was truly the outbreak for the "I'd had enough!" After I stopped crying and started to realize, there has to be something else...something more.

Here we go!! Keep up. I get THE phone call with the "we need to talk" followed by... "about some things".

So some background before I start bashing him. I was in what I thought was an amazing relationship! We, well he found me through a mutual friend and yup, he slid in my DM's. When I saw his light skinned selfie, I was like "I'm good luv, enjoy." Little did I know, I would be calling him my boyfriend for the next 3 years! We had a few bad times but the good times... you couldn't tell me that I was not going to be "Mrs. F That Nigga".

I hate the relationships where you block any signs of a break up. It's like walking outside and a bird poops in your eye...you are blindsided, literally. Well he hit me right in my heart with a left hook and I never got a chance to block. 3 minutes into this call: he's rambling on, around the bush and ultimately delivered his thesis as wanting to be "real" about "it". Another minute of empty words filled the time with him professing that he feels like he doesn't want to move on with us because he needed to get his shit together with him. This is when I began reading between the lines. "Get your shit together?" Those words didn't align to where I thought we were in our relationship. We prayed every night about his plans and my plans. We asked God to lead us in the right direction. It felt like this was because I got my blessing already and his was taking a little longer. This hurt to my core! Like he took this as me not being able to ride it out with him. To me, in my perspective and in my lens... I thought, "I support with my calls, my money, my time. Don't tell me I don't support!"

With a river of tears of confusion, I cried. I called my friend (you know, the one friend you KNOW you can call to make sure you not tripping) and she said it didn't make sense. He also wrapped it up with the classic, "Let's take a break?" Which is about the dumbest statement ever. Guys, tell me what a break is? In that moment it sounded like a break up to me. Case and point #1:

1. You don't want me to call you as much?

   1a. I'm not in the same state so I already won't be seeing you... wtf is a break. Sound like BullShit! Right?!? It was!

I called my other friend who happened to be a mutual friend. She too was confused because she had just talked to him and he said were good. I thought... "Shoot, I just seen him and we we're good!" She calls him and then calls me RIGHT back... she told him to be honest to which he said we were supposed to talk more afterwards. I thought what more would there be to say? In that moment I did remember him saying that I said, "If you wanted a break just tell me." Little did he know...and much did he misunderstand, we were referencing if he wanted to cheat...NOT THIS. What more has to be said? What more has to be done?

I was in the middle of training and I just couldn't get myself back together. Every time I looked in the mirror I cried because I just felt stupid. I was the type of girl that never did relationships. I was the "Think Like A Man," so my friends would say. My longest relationship before this was like a month and I broke it off after that. I felt like if we didn't commit and put a title on it, I couldn't get my heart broken. I couldn't feel the way I feel right now. Just melting in lies that somebody that was supposed to love me, created. My head was throbbing and 2 hours later I had to go back to training with blood-red eyeballs and still a mess! A mess mentally, emotionally, and physically! My coworkers thought somebody died, because I was no longer myself. All the while, the movie continued to play in my mind. What did I do to not be a good girlfriend? Why didn't he want to get himself together, WITH me? Together. Like we said. I came back to my hotel room and listened to Travis Greene while asking God to help me understand. That he would.

6pm rolls around and I get a call. This was the "Keep It 100" call. That last call was to throw me off and put me into a shock of devastation. This was the real reason, I was being dumped. He cheated. Yup he cheated! He kept talking around being honest and some other ish. Beat around them bushes on your own lawn, **rolls eyes** did you cheat or not?!? He said, yea. All this time, I'm sitting here talking about how these other girls are goofies and their guys are too and I'm the goofy. I mean, not too much of one because I had no idea but I mean eh what is life? You give people a chance and they go screwing you over. Lesson learned, they say. If they keep doing the same thing, when is the lesson over? Looking at my performance, I keep getting an F in relationships. An F for "Fuck Boys". I didn't cry because I didn't have any more tears. I didn't ask how many times because I really didn't care. Loved me? Please. Cared about me? Please. 3 years of talking down the drain, almost 2 years of a "committed" relationship down the drain. A waste of my TIME! And when he said he cheated, I had found my worth.

The snap back was real and quick because my savage wasn't too far in the back of my head. I think that's the problem, people get too comfortable and forget that you were once a savage. I am 26, 2 degrees, a full-time job, my own money, my own car, my own apartment, with the face of Gabrielle Union and the body of something we like to call "a SNACK!" My mass text read:

Dear Friends,

I'm officially single. I don't want to talk about it. He cheated! And that's it. So.... I'm back BITCHES!!!!!

I mean I was always the life of the party and the "fun" friend. I still have another 10 good years of being in my prime, we shall not dwell in the "Fuck Boy" madness and allow him any more of my personal precious seasons. Yea I cried, all morning. I am fine now that I have realized who I was and whose I was. Besides Savage Summer 17 had just started, might as well drive the bus!

To think, before 6pm that day...I wanted to come home, to fight for my relationship - thinking I did something wrong! HA! He knew that I wouldn't have had that many tears if he just told me he had cheated. He knew if he had told me in person I would have broken everything in sight. So, like a coward, he told me 3 days after I left to work across the country. I wouldn't have been back for another 42 days so he thought it was perfect timing for him. Lmao, the inconsiderateness cracks me up! But don't worry, I don't forget.

I would be in D.C. for another 42 days. 42 days to get my life back together before I was due back home to start a new job. Just a fresh start and the timing couldn't have been more prime. I refused to bring this baggage with me.

All night, I was texting my friends. All who did what good friends naturally do... sad at first, mixed with some supportive anger and then happy their "Faythe" was back! Planning celebrations for my homecoming, literally and figuratively! With all the encouragement and motivation from my amazing support system... I woke up saying, "God, it's Savage Szn!"

F*** That NIGGA Party!

UNEXPECTED

A friend reminded me to be careful what you ask for. I knew my prayer list was coming through and manifesting before my eyes. It's interesting how you can set your goals with someone and when your goals start to come faster than theirs... yea. The idea of "favor" isn't fair, it's just what it is. Everyone else can say I outgrew the guy but I didn't want to see myself ahead of him, in front of him, doing better than him. I don't think it was fair to him to put him on another level that I was surpassing. I still don't think it's nice when they say you're more established than he is. We were there through each other's struggles and I wanted us both around for the reaping of what we had sown. I also just always want somebody, around when it is time to enjoy things in life!

One of the things on my prayer list was to have a closer spiritual relationship with God. If I knew it would be the result of a breakup, I probably would have never put it on the list. For most of my life when things got hard I had someone there to help me get through it. When my family was going through financial struggles, I had someone. When I was abroad, I had someone. Dealing with a heart break without any family or friends to physically be there for you, I had no one. In this, I felt God drawn me near. Don't get it twisted, my support system is doing a darn good job but I can't expect them to be on call 24/7.

I don't know if showers have the same effect on other people but it can be part of my coping as well. The water feels like its rinsing the issues and struggles away. I can stand in there and just think about life, about love. Letting my body soak - hoping that any dirt, any confusion, any misunderstanding can vanish. I try to let it clear my mind. Most of the time, especially during this healing process it was too much time and my soul would pour wide open. I'd just let my emotions take over. So, now... before I cry, I pray. I pray to God thanking him first and then asking him for direction, understanding, and the drive to move forward. Sometimes I don't ask him for anything at all, I just thank him for the bad, the hurt, and f*ed up stuff in my life. I know in the moment I don't know what it means now but I know whatever happens is for a reason. It's another part of my meditation.

On that day, the one where I had my goals and plans thrown into the air, I wanted to run home! I wanted to run into the arms of people who loved me and wanted to be there for me. It was easy for me to run to them because I'm conditioned to have someone by my side when I'm going through the messy parts of life. My friend said you can't let this break you, you have a job to do! As I stayed and waited out my final days in DC, the only person I could talk to was God. The only person that would listen at any time or place of the day was God. How do you talk about God in a book that's supposed to be about being a savage? To which I answer, how can you not? Being a savage in my opinion, consists of being who you really are. I really have talks with God and I couldn't be guiding someone out of heartache if I left that part out. "Closer relationship with God!" Check

I've learned that you can't make time for everything. You work all day, have relationships and this balance gets tricky when adding in an extra "something". I thought we did make time for everything. We prayed together all the time, I just knew we were being guided together. But maybe we were praying two separate things when we weren't together.

Life is funny like that.

God is funny like that.

Maybe it wasn't really ever about me, it was about him, but then I don't want someone who doesn't think it's about US.

I can't front, he was my best friend, and I thank him for what I learned when I was with him and from the overall experience that gave me the momentum to Savage Up!

THE DISTRICT

I woke up after a long dream about that sorry cheater (we will now refer to him as such for the remainder of this tale of savagery). In the dream, our families were finally meeting. His grandma and my mom were hitting it off great - we always knew they would, because they're around the same age. That was the one-off thing or red flag about our relationship, I was barely if ever, around his family. This was matched with "I don't want them in our business."

Being in our business or your business?

Don't get me wrong, they knew who I was but they didn't know if they liked me or not. (Because they hadn't spent too much time with me.) Yet he was at my mom's house all the time, getting a plate of food, or fixing the TV. For the time we spent together, and the bond we nourished he was and will always be one of mommy's faves but again - don't get it twisted.

She gave me those motherly, always-knows-what-to- say, words of encouragement that I knew she would. The supportive reminder of how I have so much going for myself and I am such a good catch, and possibly even out of his league to begin with. She had to remind me that I was *her* daughter! Lol. Although she embraced him she offered another suggestion for my next boo. I WAS WEAK - like, mommy how have you come up with another option that quick?! It hadn't even been 24 hours! But she knows although I didn't acknowledge I had options, trust me I had options! She reassured me that since we're still young, this makes sense. It's good that he realizes he's not ready and still has to do some growing up. I didn't tell her he cheated because I didn't need her in her feelings. I also didn't need our conversation to lead into a talk about sex ...#Awkward!

24

I found that the key to helping me cope was to talk about it or keep busy. Even though I told my friends I didn't want to discuss it, the more I did, the more I was feeling normal again. Laughing at the whole conversation, it went from "I don't understand" to "I don't know how I forgot... these niggas aren't ish!" Honestly, anybody who wanted to listen would get the full story: beginning, middle and end. I had to catch myself and be mindful, making sure I wasn't killing the mood. At first I was embarrassed but I'm not ashamed anymore. Again, that plays into realizing who you are and whose you are. With it becoming a normal routine, I wake up saying God is Good! Because he truly still is! The breakup didn't take away my good genes, my good hair, my two degrees, nor my new job! It made me sad but at the end of every day, it just was what it was. What was a challenge was when I'd have nothing to do, no one to talk to and had to really sit and soak-in the situation, by myself. The hotel we were staying at, had a delay in which we waited three hours to fully get checked in. You guessed it, those 3 hours were spent with that Break-Up movie playing on repeat in my mind. With the help of some Travis Greene, I got through it.

Anytime I am alone and I am feeling overwhelmed about everything, Gospel music just clears my mind. Normally, I would turn to some Lauryn Hill but I think she makes me more emotional rather than empowered. Gospel fills my spirit and solidifies whose I am. I am God's! I am his child and I am still and forever will be his.

Now what shows me who I am... lol. What time y'all tryna drink?!

So of course, I had to involve my own drug of choice into this element. "Don't drink you're going to cry and be sad!" Girl. AND!? Lmao. I wanted to feel as normal as possible, as quick as possible and it's something I normally indulge in. I indulged less when I was in a relationship so my plan was rooted in...let me gone head and rebuild that tolerance. Before the drinks start flowing'... it's nothing like getting all dolled up to make you feel like you can take on the world!

I went and got my makeup box and took over the bathroom. Eyebrows on point! Highlight poppin! Lip plumper got me channeling my inner Megan Good. Wig LAID! **Puts on my full spaghetti strap one piece with my cute satin sneakers.** Rose gold watch matched with a choker and some hoops.

I stepped back from the mirror and laid eyes upon the work I'd just put in…

BISH! YOU CUTE! And I hadn't even put on my lashes, you know that's what turns it all the way up!

Admiring the masterpiece that reflected back from the mirror, now this is truly what reminds me WHO I AM!

Oh wait, I almost forgot to give the utmost thanks and appreciation (close your eyes and bow your head as I lead us into prayer):

I would just like to thank the makeup gods for allowing me to beat my face and I pray that my primer, translucent powder, and finishing spray all hold hands at the table of not letting my face slide by the end of the night. In Mac's Name, amen. While we at it…

I would also like the wig gods for allowing my lace front to be snatched, bleached, tinted and plucked in all the right places. I would like my clips and the hair gods to hold hands at the table of China's finest wig collections and not allow my lace wig to slide off by the end of the night. In the name of baby hairs laying, amen.

So… the night was young! The lyft prices were high and I was on my way to the bars. It kicked off with a political conversation in the car with my driver. Sir, don't piss on my spirit with talk about Donald Trump RIGHT before I have to go see the whites. He drops me off in front of this bar, peeking out the window…I think "Oh ok, so everybody just gone walk in and out looking like they didn't care today?" It was raining but geesh.

Waiting on an old coworker I decided to explore a few more bars. I went into another hole in the wall and knew that was not it! Making my way back towards the entrance, I'm screaming from my core…"Come on D.C., y'all claim y'all summers are better than Chicago, let me see something that's gone prove it!" I guess Fridays nights in the Chi can be a tad dry as well. I know this whole past year, my Friday nights consisting of passing out in my bed and waiting for Saturday morning to begin my weekend! Between 2 jobs and having a boyfriend to attend to, I was always exhausted by Friday. Maybe everybody else is the same way?

My coworker calls me, I hear my name being yelled over the chatter and decent music playing overhead - I turn around to meet her. We hear some "Future" playing from down the rain soaked street and we KNEW this was the place to be. As we're walking towards the bar, picking up our pace as the melodies pull us closer, leaning out of the car is something carmel looking my way. He yells out to get my attention and based on his rims I'm thinking…let's see what this one is about. He asks how I'm doing and I ask where the spots are around here, he says he isn't sure and I walk off. As he rolls up his window confused, I check the stats: 1 point for me and 0 for these niggas. I'm not here to be your friend this summer my goal is to make me feel better about myself. Now I know that ultimate "insecurities theory": only people who are insecure about themselves have to tear others down in order to make them feel better… You *damn* right! I had 42 days and any boost that says "Bish you still got it!" I AM HERE FOR IT!

Finally, in the bar, the women are cute but the guys…eh. Wow. I left Chicago for this?!

I wasn't anticipating looking for a replacement while I was there so I decided to chill. The shots were lining up, the drinks were flowing and it was turning into a great night. We leave the bar and it's time for Hookah! I am by no means a smoker but Hookah is LIFE! We sit down in a dimly lit section, perfect

Hookah environment. On my right are three big booty joints sitting on the side and this is a sure fire sign I'm in the right place. I know these are my type of females! I appreciate a female that goes out and she f's it up each time. Translation: Every time this young lady goes out for a night of fun she is always very put together!

We hookah and the hour mark begins to pass. They start playing my song and the night is complete! That one song that just signals, if the night ended right now...this journey through the rain was worth it! Something about that Memphis freestyle gave me all types of real nigga vibes. And yet, music is how "we" bonded. Yea, me and the ex. I think...as I order another comforting shot, "Whelp it's over now". I was good all night long, enjoying myself all the way up until we got to Ben's Chili Bowl. They had a John Legend song playing in the bathroom and my whole demeanor changes. The power of music. I got sad and low-key wanted to shed a few tears. I remained strong... I sucked it up and went back in line to get my chili cheese fries.

While waiting for my cab outside, here comes the whites. (I do love my white people, so "the whites" is not a term to offend caucasians as a whole, rather to group them when they do something only white people do). Exhibit A: This white guy walks up to me and tries to put his hand in my food with the "let me get some" face. Now, you know black people don't play that putting your hand in their food. I don't know who raised him but it clearly wasn't somebody who was popped for touching someone else's plate. I said kindly, "sir, back away from me". Another black guy we were with asked him the same thing. Now, remember I'm already emotional and low-key angry because that's the part of intoxication I am at, at this point. He walks away then comes back around trying to play with me, as if he did not just disrespect my plate of drunken fries. Quickly, I do a reflection of sorts with some addition thrown in, trying to tally how many people I have that could bail me out of jail for knocking this white boy's teeth back? I wish the night would just end there.

My driver does what all rideshare drivers do, you know...the constant calling as if he's been waiting for hours, he asks, "Where you at?". Immediately I think, "Ummmm excuse you? Who do you think you talking to? I'm not your friend nor your homie!" He drives up and his front seats are so far back! They're practically back seats at this distance. I'm struggling to help him push one up, eventually I give up and just sit in the front. I hop in the car and immediately let him know he had terrible customer service! "Did you think I was black or something?" "Did you think you knew me?" Lord help this brother do better! Of course, he indulges in this part of the conversation, to finish off my frustration or add to it...he asks if I had a man... #AnnoyedAlready

I told him I had just got out of a relationship, remember any chance I got to vent, I took. He proceeded to ask if I want him to make me feel better about it. Which is when things started to get weird. This sounded more like stranger danger (the one they taught us in grade school), especially when he missed the same exit twice and tried handing me his bottle of Remy! Oh no! My luck with the stars is not this bad, I am not getting cheated on, dumped, and raped all in the same week! God forbid this is how I'm going to die! Very politely or as politely as one can be at 2am...I told aforementioned stranger, "Sir, you have one job and that's to take me back to the hotel." He looked over at me...I continued, "...this ride was only supposed to be $10, it is now $20! All this talking has you distracted, missing exits...will you be financing this ride?" We finally get to the hotel and I asked him again if he'd be the one funding this ride? He clearly thought I was joking, when I told him I want my money. I step out of the car and he calls after me stating he'd pay for the ride if I gave him my number. SO...as most women do, I passed him my go-to fake number. He reaches in his pockets to discover, of course has no cash. Boy Bye! I CAN NOT! Since he ruined my night I had to even the score, because you can't be allowed to drive offering people Remy! I made sure to add that into my review!

UGH!

10 drunken hate texts, 1 unanswered FaceTime, and I sat on the floor in the hallway. I knew I was still low-key spinning so I did not want to lay down, quite yet because I knew I might get sick. I called my friend Lex, and she was up... after about 45 minutes of just venting, I was done.

Thanks Lex I needed you that night!

COPE WITH ME

So, this is going to be harder than I thought; don't forget...I was recovering in another state without my friends or family. None of my coworkers were really dedicated to what my therapy plan looked like or my post-breakup 911 journey. Everything pointed to me being the only one interested in the "turn-up" life. Reason #63825, DC summer doesn't measure up to SummertimeCHi... my friends there would be in "turn-up" mode from Thursday evening through Sunday evening! Instant flashbacks of my pre-girlfriend weeks, I just had to go into retirement early to be a good significant other and look where that got me. Regardless, I was back. In full effect, ready to make this lifestyle adjustment in the name of healing. I had gotten in the habit of going out by myself, trying to make the most of DC, bringing a taste of home to my temporary summer hiatus. Nobody wants to go out by themselves because you're going to look like a loser! Lmao. Don't get me wrong - I don't need a group of people to have fun, ask my friends I make my own fun! But I don't want to be at the bar, in a city where I only know a few people by myself. It's not safe and I'm not about that life!

In my rekindled savage ways, I found myself often thinking...Am I going to date again? I wasn't even ready to hand out my number. Even the mere thought of a guy made me sick and uneasy. It had to have been a "Boris Kodjoe" walking around the corner for me to actually put effort into the flirting game. A guy tried to dance with me at the club and I was like chill... He also wasn't that cute either but I was just like ew-don't touch me! Pause- I know select readers are reading and patiently waiting for me to throw in details of me laid up with 3 different types of guys and committing to being like a "f boy". But ....mmmm the way our will is set up, my family don't play that. And that's just not what happened. I didn't want sex to be a way of getting back at someone who probably won't even read this book. I also didn't see a purpose in making a man happy or benefiting from my trauma. That just didn't make sense to me, so no you won't get that here. What you will get is the POWER! The power I didn't know I still had, I found it and would never forget I had it again!

I also value the tradition of being private about what is happening in your relationship.

MMMMM how am I being private and I am writing a whole book about how I got cheated on and dumped (I can't just say one without the other). I need some therapeutic writing and you all need a good laugh, with some advice as well so I am going to write as long as you all will continue to read! **Thanks, love ya!**

But I think that all of this is good in a way. I went into a long-term relationship, not knowing what to expect because I had never been in one. So, when it ended, I had no idea how to deal with it. I kept asking myself what am I supposed to do? And I kept asking God to just help me understand. So many people deal with it in different ways and I have been fortunate enough to have the ability to already have found my mode of coping. Some people fall into a mode of depression. I thought I would too. I thought I wouldn't be able to manage through the summer and was very adamant about returning home. Just quitting, because I thought I couldn't handle this on my own. By day 7, week 1...I found myself still there, figuring out life, myself and the world I was creating. I mean this was nothing compared to China insert **Sleep Emoji**!

Update: which may be seen as a moment of weakness...I did snap him on night 7 to see if he would snap back...and he did, with the "You Look Good". I knew that already, that's why I snapped, literally and figuratively! By this point I had changed his name to B**** in my phone. This has no effect, it just made me feel better when I see it. I hadn't fully deleted pictures. Thanks to the latest Apple update they were still in my recently deleted photos but when I knew once I got there, to that magic land at the end of my season... I would delete them. I would change his name back, and eventually just delete his number altogether. Getting rid of the memories is harder than trying not to curse him out every day, honestly. So many photos and videos, I documented everything because I knew I would need them in our wedding. We would have a slideshow of embarrassing moments...

MMMKAY, back to reality! Why didn't y'all slap me real quick? I hope someone is reading and has said aloud "SHUT UP SIS!! AIN'T NO WEDDING AND AIN'T NO MEMORIES! HE CHEATED AND DUMPED YA!" AHHHHHHHH LMAO, my friends are so mean I love y'all!

THE REBIRTH

D.C. and I were much like a bad relationship. It kept telling me that it didn't want me there and I stayed. Every year something drastic happens... when I say drastic I mean highly irritating to the normal person. Ordering a new phone and the next day cracking the entire screen of the new phone, it's not the end of the world situations but I swear things that annoy me ONLY seem to happen when I'm in D.C.

Exhibit A, summer of 2017 was just one of many.

I received a phone call from an old friend that had heard about my death...not my Aunt Daisy but the death of my new-found relationship. Not that I'm not surprised word had gotten around, that's probably one of the most irritating things of the breakup though, constantly having to talk about it when new people, that you didn't want to tell find out. She was very compassionate because she could relate. She too had been done dirty for many years with her significant other and the moral of her story was to not go back. Did I think about going back...? TO lie or to not lie...? I did. Not right then, and don't call me crazy but I thought that maybe in 10 years he would change. I still loved him. I do. At this point it had been almost a month and I still saw us together. I never thought I would feel like this. I was always that girl that told my friends, these guys don't change and once a cheater always a cheater. And here I was, contemplating about returning to the B.S. What type of spell is this?!

It took a friend from my childhood to bring light into my world and shake up the trance of the spell I was in. She told me the same exact thing that her guy told her was the same things mine would tell me.It was almost like dating the same character. I never compared her life to mine, although I knew her relationship was similar just on a longer and more intense scale. She basically told me to look at her life and if I went back to him, this is what it

34

would be. Don't get me wrong - she's doing very well for herself financially but the heartbreaks and rollercoasters, my stomach could never handle. Did I want her life? I didn't. My ex told me I didn't deserve him and I deserve someone better than him. Classic - I thought. She told me her guy told her the same thing over and over and she wouldn't listen. In me allowing him to dictate what was "ok" and what wasn't, was unfair. In saying that, she said he lowered the expectation bar and made everything "ok". He let the girl he cheated on her with know it was ok too, because she now knew about her. So if it happened again, it would be "ok".

Every year I come back to D.C. and BS ensues, that shows me all the signs that I was just ready to go back home. My career was there in DC and I could make a good living. However, DC had never shown me that it was supposed to be my home....

When I say DC just never let me be great, bruh listen to this!

Y'all ready to laugh? I am about to embarrass myself for your entertainment because I honestly can't do anything but laugh. Here we go! Keep up.

I'm in the middle of National Mall on an outing with my scholars and had my fingers crossed, hoping to find a coffee spot that I could just chill and write at. I brought my charger and I hadn't written anything in a minute, I was just ready to knock out some pages. I see a place, dash inside and immediately hit the bathroom! My headphones are in and I'm on the phone just talking away, per usual. I sat my phone down on the tissue dispenser, with the headphones still in my ear...carrying on my conversation. I start to pull my shorts down and as soon as I start pee, my phone drops in the toilet! I immediately try to fish my phone out. You know how field trips go, limited time to do normal human functions so by this point I had to go REALLY bad. I couldn't stop peeing. My shorts weren't even all the way down so not only am I peeing on my arm that's reaching to get my phone out of the toilet, I had piss on my shorts and my panties. WTF is LIFE!?!

I swear to you I thought I was BACK IN CHINA!!! FOR THOSE OF YOU THOSE OF YOU WHO ARE LOST AT THIS COMMENT, READ BLKGIRLNCHINA!

I was in this Starbucks, I'm wet, my clothes are wet, my phone is done, I had to think REAL quick! I pull my shorts back up and wrap my button up shirt that was over my tank top around my waist. I knew there was a TJ Maxx somewhere within the next few blocks so I take my bag and start walking. I pick up my pace with every step. It was sunny outside so my shorts *were* drying but not only did I feel disgusting, I could smell the urine! WTF is LIFE!?!?

ONLY IN D.C. DO I NOT ONLY DROP MY PHONE IN THE TOILET BUT I'VE PEED ON MYSELF LIKE A CHILD AND I AM WALKING THE STREETS OF D.C. SMELLING LIKE PISS!

Every year, D.C. tells me stop coming back! Every summer I kept bringing my butt back! Like what else has to be done to realize, this place is not for you! No good vibes! I never really had a good time out there; the money was good but I kept asking myself, WHAT ARE YOU DOING?!

I get to an intersection and spy the promised land at the next block. I finally run into a Walgreens and grab baby wipes. I come out, still wet...and spot a Forever 21,dash in to find a cheap dress and panties and head to the line. Y'all...the line was long af! Of course. I'd found myself standing in line smelling like piss!!!! D.C. don't do me like this! D.C. says "but I told you... I told you and you didn't listen!" I pay for my stuff, find a bathroom and I'm able to clean myself off and change my clothes. Side Note: I still feel dirty, I need a shower and a foot massage for this whole hour I just dedicated to my life being in SHAMBLES!

Just like D.C., I can't go back and I won't. It took some pissy clothes and an old friend to let me erase the whole idea completely out of my mind.

THANKS, POOH!

NEW PHONE, WHO DIS?

I wonder if God is looked at my last post and sent Jesus a text like "LMFAO!"
My friend told me that things tend to come in 3's and I hoped that last incident was the third installment in the catastrophe series happening in D.C.

It's pretty amazing when you start to reflect back on things, you see the purpose in everything. Being in another state, I didn't have to drive past my ex's house or worry about running into him, but my phone was like a capsule of the love that we once had. So many pictures, so many videos that I kept from the beginning all the way up till days before it would be the ending to all of it. Every time I opened up my Snap, he was there in my memories, he was there in my text messages, just reminders of confusion. I called myself trying to delete some of them but they didn't do anything but end up in my recently deleted photo gallery, I couldn't do it on my own.

A T-Mobile store happened to be right around the corner the day I dropped my phone in the Starbucks toilet. I asked the customer service rep what my options were for a replacement. He relievingly told me I had insurance so I could have a new one mailed to me by next week. Problem: I was leaving from New York the next morning and I was working, I needed something now! He told me my phone was already paid for and I would be able to upgrade for the low if I wanted to, today. I didn't have much time to decide because I had to get back to our bus so I told them give me the new phone.

They wouldn't be able to backup my new phone so everything in that phone would just stay where it was at. I realized that's the way I wanted it. It's a song that says, "Take everything, I don't want it, I don't need it God, I just want you" by Travis Greene. It seems like once I *realized* going back was no longer an option, God pushed me an extra step and threw away my old life. I didn't want any of my contacts, my old text messages, I didn't want to be held captive by a life that no longer deserved the woman I have become. A life that no longer served me. As drastic as it is to just start over, I felt cleansed. It was like that shower I took the night of the pissy tragedy, I felt refreshed. I am a new person without someone by my side, I have to think, act and carry myself as a new person in a new and better light if I wanted to just let it go! God said you playing with yourself with that old phone. He knew I was waiting to scroll back too far accidently in my camera roll. To accidentally cross those pictures to provide me a quick moment to reflect on a good memory. God said make new memories in a new chapter and that's what I intend to do.

Literally, NEW PHONE...WHO DIS?

THE REBOUND

What I didn't want to do with this was to embarrass him or make him feel like his position in my life was nothing more than a way to get over somebody else. I would be lying to myself to think that he was not a major component in my "getting over" the ex.

Oh Brooklyn meshed with the fond memories of having that type of love, that was very familiar in my house. My parents met in Brooklyn, got married in Brooklyn, and somehow I thought that maybe Brooklyn wasn't such a bad idea. Thus, when the opportunity of an old boo presented himself in my DM, I thought that maybe this would actually be a great time to rekindle.

To know me, you know who lives in Brooklyn. He knows, as soon as he reads this, I'm talking about us. Yes, us. Before there was anybody else that mattered in my college+ years, he was the first and we were US. It wasn't hard to get back in sync like nothing had ever fell off. Although, it was actually eight years (to be exact) since I had seen him, I go to Brooklyn almost every year to see my grandmother and every time I think that maybe I'll run into him. Never did.

Just like a scripted scene from my favorite show, *Sex and the City*, it was a magical night in the streets of New York City. We had so much to catch up on, and found ourselves across the table from each other at a cute Mexican restaurant. (Y'all already know, he ain't seen me in 8 years and I was in my thick days, I was out here looking like a WHOLE MEAL! If we used to be together and now we not no more, im showing up, *every time*, to make sure you understand I'm the one you'll regret.)

I asked about his ex and what happened. The candle placed in the middle of our table, separating us continued to flicker. He started comparing the levels of trust that lacked in their relationship, compared to when we were together. (Mmmm you said she wasn't me... but we already knew that! BUT-talk about trust, I'm too trusting!) He continued with how he couldn't take the extraness ranging from checking phones to watching his every move. Small arguments that turned into large stalemate battles. He was used to someone (me) that showed him we were better than that detective work. Like I have said before, that's not me. So am I rare? Extremely!

We stroll down to Dumbo Park - talk about romance, and the scene being perfectly set! I'm here for it - Holding my purse, walking on the outside of the streets, IT'S THE LITTLE THINGS THAT COUNT!!! We were gazing at each other under the Manhattan lights that glared from across the river. My ex, who? (*I'm going to thank God a lot in this book, but geesh, he sure allows you to have just some good feeling moments in your life, through all the BS reality throws at you.*) For just those 4 hours with someone I haven't seen in years, I was truly in a happy moment. And that is okay! Many times we will go through a difficult state and feel that we're not allowed to enjoy life or be happy until we are out of our struggles. Who knows how long you're meant to be in the position you're in and learning that lesson? For me, it genuinely gave me motivation to keep pushing. It reminded me that I could still feel something that wasn't hatred or sadness in my heart. I still had the ability to have emotions that didn't have ANYTHING to do with my previous situation.

(Y'all know how you remembered you had some fruit snacks in your pocket while you were taking that standardized test? Brooklyn wasn't my rebound but he was my fruit snack. Someone, a friendly and comforting reminder to be like "yo shorty, you good!")

It was also certain things that he did, I didn't realize I cared about, until he did them. This happened a lot during Savage Szn.

During my short stay in NY, I got a chance to meet Brooklyn's mom. You would've thought I was receiving a lifetime achievement award the way he was doing this introduction. I didn't get a chance to get a word in, I just sat back and listened. *insert hovering thought bubble above my head* So this is what happens when they really like you? Most guys will vouch: when you meet moms, you're someone that is going to be around. Now, with *these* good looks, standout resume and all that, I am usually the girl who meets the mom. However, I have never had someone go on and on about my greatness and why I am such a great person.

(Come through Savage Szn, y'all out here cutting up!!! Got a girl feeling like she a Queen for real!!)

Let's be very clear though, for review...once I remembered my worth, I was able to allow and understand when someone else knew it as well. Only then was I able to appreciate what a "rebound" was for me.

His response in his pre-reading this: **Disclaimer, he's fluent in Hopeless Romantic, so it's about to get REAL and intimate at the same time! Lmao

"I first want to say this is beautiful and I enjoyed reading this, even though I think you should call me "Game-Winning Rebound". LOL...But one thing that stood out the most and is 100% accurate is regretting you. Trying to find that connection like we had is like trying to find another Faythe Missick (Literally) which is impossible!

{I BE TRYNA TELL THEM, YOU WILL NEVER FIND ANOTHER!!!! Ok back to him lol}

I've been single for two years now and you'd think I would be hard pressed trying to get you but I'm stuck between wanting to keep in contact, but not trying to waste your time. No matter if I was a rebound or not, what we had was magic. I truly miss you and love you dearly. I will always be that "Brother from Brooklyn" in ya eyes and I can live with that. That night we linked up for tacos with them watered down drinks and the avocado man putting in work trying to make you laugh lol. Walking side by side, holding your hand, cursing out the cab driver for looking too long cuz you WAS looking like "A WHOLE MEAL". More like a garden because you are the type to nurture and care. You are fucking amazing Faythe! You will find happiness and peace of mind, IDC if it's with me or not. You deserve everything this world has to offer!" {In my Mama D voice, I DESERVE! LMAO}

He so unnecessarily stroked my ego but I mean it's not like he's not telling the truth! Lmao.

Not specifically with Brooklyn and I's situation but Jesus I see the same thing happen again and again. The thirst to get you and then they get you and then the CUT OFF GAME is STRONG. Then the regrets roll in. Guys do me a favor and just save yourself some time and dignity. I'm far from perfect but being a loyal and gorgeous woman that's a good ass time, I AM THAT!

(This is why God didn't give me all that body that I ask for when I eat my Popeyes because it would just be too much for these guys and myself to HANDLE!! And those who can relate, you understand the struggle.)

EFFECTIVE

"I'm about to put an end to Savage Szn."

The most common phrase amongst all of the Savage Szn men that have been a part of this eat, pray and party movement. The stories that came out of my 7 month season allowed me to opened my mind and my "type" to explore different options.

As things seemed to have come to an end, I was at a point in asking myself what am I doing? What do I really want? In those 7 months and roughly 28 weeks, I dated. I only wanted to date and was not interested in anything serious. However, when something came and confronted me, I was in the moment and I liked it! I liked it until the honeymoon phase of the situation was ending, and the struggles of being in a relationship, compromising and dealing with a person because you are hoping to grow with them come about. A new set of questions had me reflecting... What have you gotten yourself into? What do you really want? And how is this going to affect the people who are involved, who have invested their time and their energy into building something. I did not have to know what I wanted for myself but it was not fair to not to be able to express my emotions and feelings when others become involved. That there, is growth.

The idea of working on me, I felt I lost it. Caught up in playing house and the romance, I love it. I don't watch Sex and the City just for the fashion but the spinning of my emotions when you look into each other's eyes and feel the realness of the moment. Is it just a moment? In the back of my mind I was keeping myself unattached and prepared for a "fuck up" to happen because I still didn't know what I wanted. My plan I thought, was to take things slowly until I did figure it out. There comes a time when life speeds up, three months can feel like three years and I couldn't just let go, "This is not going to be a breeze." Although I felt that somewhere in the cracks of it all, I lost sight of what was real and what was fantasy. Not so savage...here.

What was real? Compromising, I thought I would compromise more. That feeling of choosing what battle to surrender to went against things I stood for. I put up the wall against who I selected to create an opportunity with. Had I compromised too much? Was I really okay dating someone out of my faith? Was I okay with dating someone with kids? I thought because I played my cards right before that it didn't matter what I thought I wanted because what was what I wanted broke my heart. I made a vow to no longer be restricted to what I thought my *type* was. I was exploring. And when I explored a little too deep, I did not know where I was.

THE MIDDLE EAST

I'm convinced this man had and still has a second family on the side. Not only do I believe he has a second family on the side, I am convinced she's a beautiful black queen and he wants me to be the mistress.

Never take a guy you meet in the club seriously. The exception I gave myself here was that in pursuing a line-up of eligible men... it doesn't hurt to notice the section of Arab money guys gracing the bar.

The night started off pretty dry. My friend invited me to a kickback at one of her boo's humble abodes filled with old Africans with gold teeth. Now if you know me you know I love my African men from Naija to the Congo #HereForIt! However, THIS party was not worth the following: my time, my slayed wig, nor my beat face. But as a friend, I will always be supportive when my friend needs me to be that, "So...where your friends at?" I come through with these good looks and conversation to entertain. Now do know this is the single me talking because when I have a man, I don't have nothing for you, sis.

So with the party being dry, there are still shots on the table and ample opportunity for an after party to take place. I can pregame here, and hit a real party with some real excitement afterwards. With Savage Szn at an all time high, I was at the exact slim thick size I was aiming to be at. I probably would've taken more pictures if I knew it was going to be gone within the next few months. (Fast metabolism and dancing twice a week and I'm back sitting with the skinny team). But that night I had on the "Faythe Special", as my friends would say. I love a good bodysuit and a jean jacket with some heels. Basic and comfy was much easier to pull off when your body is poppin! After getting a little tipsy we finally were ready to leave. Four of us started to get in the uber and here come the oldies trying to get a number and invite themselves to part two of the night. The Uber driver demanded non-riding riders to back up so he could pull off... YASSS 10-points for Abdul because yall, they had more than enough of my time.

The destination was River North. I was in the mood for the bars and ultimately to find a nice diverse crowd. Hoping to find some "corporate black men" led the agenda for the night. As we hopped out of the Uber I first saw security staring our way, second I spot the never-ending line down the block. What does a savage do, in savage szn? Of course I engaged in conversation with the two men working security. Sadly enough, I just didn't see that "one in, one out" 20+ minute waste of standing in line time. You know the scene in "Knocked Up" with Katherine Heigl, she's at the club with her sister and they walk right in, it was kind of like that. We walked right in as one should always be doing. I can't lie Savage Szn has gotten me quite spoiled because although I am not opposed to a line, I've gotten accustomed to walking past it. *Lawrence is to blame lol.

We're in there and a group of guys made their way over to us. Eh not really my type, talking about they're from Ohio and a tad older… but then they had their friend. The overly intoxicated and wants to entertain type. Ugh - I just knew that night would have been an absolute waste if I was in this circle with these guys all night. As I got my friend (who was far less intoxicated than the man attempting to entertain us) to sober up, we quickly moved around. We move around to other side of bar. Then I see what I'll call a Middle Eastern prince to sweep me off my feet from a far. Is it a bird, is it a plane, oh no so much better AN ARABIAN SNACK! Normally, I take one for the team and make the first move, but I patiently waited to feel out his vibe and make sure he knew he would have to show interest if he wanted me. After a few more hours at the club, Saturday became Monday and we were on our first date.

He shows up three hours late….mmmm I should have known then. With calls expressing that he was running late from work but still coming if I was open. The old me would have took my butt right to sleep but this was what I thought this dating life would bring. I expected some compromise. New things that I may not be used to but if I am patient they might have been worth it. I

46

thought it was. I can't lie I thought I was about to hit the jackpot. Now with money not being everything, I look for in a man, it didn't matter because he was loaded. As a retired pro-athlete and Arab Money written on his forehead it was not only on his forehead but in his bank account, in his private jet, and I saw it ALL in my future. Let me tell you the devil was like "BIITCCHHH DON'T TWEAK!" I just knew all the headaches of dating in my previous situation was worth it because I was about to become a Middle Eastern princess. He's Muslim which was different for me because with my father being a Pastor, I am big on religion. I was open to new interests and plus I was about to be a princess. God would understand.

Well if you're reading this, you already know that didn't happen because I surely wouldn't be writing this book. I'd be sitting pretty doing nothing on an island disappeared on mfs.

Y'all asked how I messed this up? Please go back to the beginning of this section and read the first lines. When I say I am convinced he had another life... Has to!! Don't argue with me on this one.

After our date, I never saw him again. If I had to guess, he had sent me off approximately twelve times. It's like clockwork and it's crazy af. I was pissed after the second time and then I just got used to it. Conversations were great! And then he would be like, "Babe I want to see you!" He schedules the time and like an hour before we're supposed to meet he just goes MIA. Like doesn't answer the phone and a response to a text is far too much to ask. It's like clockwork. I had come to an internal agreement that I more so needed his financial coaching. Then he'd be able to continue his game of cat and mouse. Although, I was sure I could find somebody else to give me insight on how to get to invest and secure the money. I was just amused and thought it was hilarious the way our situation continued to develop. Every two to three weeks, I got some form of communication. Either a text or we'd have a long phone conversation, it ends with "I want to see you tomorrow", tomorrow came and went and I'd never see him! What in the hell?! Maybe he using me for good conversation too? It's like every time he made plans his wife was like, "Baby, I'm ovulating. Where you going?!"

Look sis whomever you are I don't blame you. Y'all gon have some beautiful babies and you will never have to work a day in your life! I mean he still watches my snaps faithfully and still calls me on his regular schedule but don't let me get in the way your dreams and aspirations.

As "live" as my life looks from social media, from what I have been told, this lifestyle comes with some crazy situations. But I was open to just living.

CONVENIENCE

Out of the friend zone, in comes our next suitor. Of course you have people that you honestly don't think will make sense, but for the moment he did. I would like to introduce, Mr. Convenient. "Viva La Savage Szn", I realize now that at this point I never really enjoyed just the company of myself all the damn time because at the end of the day, I love good company. This particular company is one that has come with many interests and ideas that challenge who I am as a person. When I say opposites attract, they definitely do for us. I am faith and he is physical. I never knew how much I relied on how I felt, being a guide for my life.

A lot of people wouldn't even consider the opposites attract idea, specifically people rarely consider others who challenge the way you think. In our situation, it was in the questioning of it all that made me have a better understanding of what is real. Our opposites follow below.

1. Religion
Our most controversial conversation were rooted in our faith. With him growing up in a church and being so deep into his faith, it took a college history class for that to be challenged. I on the other hand, grew up in the church and til this day, I can not front and say that. Being a believer of God is the STRUGGLE! My father who I see as a reflection of purity has been shamed, embarrassed and hurt by the church. I have seen many things that tell me, you know what, you can pray at home. As I grow up and go through my own life experiences, I am content with sitting in my customs and the religious family culture that I grew up in. For everything else, specifically, religion is very individualistic for me. Why do we need religion if it has been a root of many evil things that have transpired in our world? Specifically as a tool for oppression. How do we still breathe life into something that has been used to put us in a system of bigotry and turmoil because of the color of our skin?... Because I do not have the strength to govern myself accordingly without the guidance of what is right and

what is wrong. People who believe in nothing are something dangerous. You could say that I am in between Locke and Hobbes. I believe that people are entitled to individual freedom but I believe that we are born selfish. My faith is what keeps me grounded and genuinely heartfelt for people around to me to prosper in life. My religion allows me to know what happiness feels like or at least have an idea. It gives me a peace of mind. And you know what, I just would rather not run around like a crazy person worrying about any and every thing because I can just lean on God trusting that what's for me is for me because he said it's so. For me, it makes life easier.

He can't see love but I can because my faith let's me know what it feels like from God.

With many complicated conversations, the company is quite enjoyable. As we start closing out cuffing season and moving into SummerTime Chi, I had a question for him. I even knew when I thought about it, he would not have the answer. He thinks everything has a bridge and when you get there you will cross it, but as proactive as I am with my button to move a guy around if I sense that I am getting too deep, I can tell when or if I will eventually have a safe surface under my feet...(it's usually 3 months and they have to go). No but seriously, I know 3 months is when I start to get very emotionally attached. It sucks to say that I like convenience and I see myself starting to fall. I constantly repeat in my head that this isn't going to last long so that I can convince myself, don't tweak!

A gem that one of my exes noted was, "Don't have too much of a wall up though... that's how you scare away the people that are supposed to stay." How ironic of him to say that, I never even built that wall for him and that ended in a tragic disaster of many heartaches and just goofiness in college. I do agree that I can not keep the Savage Szn going forever because I am more of a Carrie Bradshaw than a Samantha (referencing again my favorite show Sex and the

City). Although I am very good at being Samantha, it's not always where I necessarily want to be in life.

The question was, "Am I just convenient?" He just moved here and I told him that he really hasn't had a chance to see what Chicago has to offer. Honestly, if you haven't experienced Summertime Chi yet, you haven't seen what life has to offer. The amount of life that is moving for those 3 months, June, July, and August. People deal with the terrible Siberian winters, so we can enjoy the amazing summers. Day parties, nightlife, sundresses, and VIP!

BTW I am quite tired of the mads being upset that you have to wait in line at the door. Then when I walk in, you have a smart comment to say. You standing in line is a lifestyle that you choose, I choose to walk past the line and walk right in. If you haven't figured out how it's done then I advise you to take notes rather than being mad cause you have to stand with the common people. It's not like you're going to be in a section anyway, so what's to be upset about when you were born to be in General Admission…?

Alright - let's carry on where we left off, convenience. I asked him if I was convenient for him. And of course, he always gave an even vaguer answer, which I figured and accepted. At the exact moment when I asked, he really didn't understand the question. Not realizing the type of situation he was in, and the draft that he was about to walk in when the weather broke. He's lost in my concern. I really didn't need an answer because I was simply talking out loud, note that I was preparing myself for the finale of something real cute and convenient for me as well. Now although, I strive to drop my job and be a housewife and live happily ever after - daily, I naturally am always thinking about myself as well. If I was going to suffer or be embarrassed, I could no longer subscribe to it. I was not sitting around waiting until June to set myself up for the okie-doke - that just didn't make sense. Frankly, it would just be poor planning. What sucked was that honestly, he made a lot of sense for me. Buuuuuut - welp not about to figure that one out today! Or for this go around with Mr. Convenience. As stated earlier, faithfully...what's for you is for you and I will always stand behind that.

With a good friend who moved back into the city, he finally realized what I meant by my question. We go out and go back to his friend's apartment... I step into this State St luxury home and can see the entire city, from Navy Pier to the Field Museum. The first thing I say to him AND his friend, "The amount of females that y'all are about to take down because of this view, you have no idea!" Y'all, I watched sun rises, while cuddling in the corner of windows that put a frame around the view. It was so damn magical. I just knew Mickey and Minnie were going to start floating on clouds outside. Harry Potter just running across buildings zapping niggas and Cupid would run to the window and shoot throw my heart connecting us.

THIS IS NOT GOING TO BE A BREEZE!

When I said what I said, he told me in that moment he finally understood what I was talking about. He was confused his damn self, at the opportunity that had been placed on the table. Whether it was his apartment or not, it's only two of them there, it is about to be the ultimate thot location. From my experience, Chicago has a very entertainment lifestyle vibe. Especially when it comes to nice things, and especially when it's black professionals living this vibe. Girls...they are a rare breed and I just took it as there being hope! Faith. Now whether this hope included him acting right, and this being my new potential luxury lifestyle...he was still becoming bae. You see, me trying figure out when I was going to glide out got tricky. I just can't wait in a position where I don't know if I am just here for convenience and sheer ignorance of what all Summertime Chi promises. A city that never breaks its promise during the warmer months.

It's not even just with relationships, it's with life. Are we doing things that are convenient or just makes sense for now. The amount of possibilities are crazy.

52

It's a feeling of being content. With convenience, it brings ease, it comes with the ability to just move at a comforting pace. There is nothing "extra" about it. Where it becomes difficult is trying to figure out, what exactly you are doing? Is this where I want to be in life, is it a smaller breakdown of comfortability? I just needed to move one or two things around to secure that happiness. Well what the hell was the happiness, where are we going. What is real?

Okay - let's take a step back because I don't want to overwhelm you. You should constantly be thinking about growth and what next steps are in development. We are a system and the system has to continue to work. Faythe, the business is a flourishing rise to a place of peace of mind. Well I guess if you believe you're always supposed to work on Earth and then rest in heaven then, we work. Nonetheless, I think God made us complex and things can't just be black and white because we are so vast and so different. Even with language and meaning of the term: convenient. The connotation is automatically often negative. If I change my words and say that it's an opportunity for growth, a step towards greatness, even if him and I part ways... it was a great time!

I was asking if I was convenient for him to gauge what those next steps were. To be proactive with how much energy and time I was pouring in this. I also wanted to keep him around without being around because just having him around would be a LITTy situation for me. I was more than aware of that. I play chess - so when I move, don't always think it's defensive. I can't be the girl not getting invited to the party because we used to talk. I still want to reap the benefits too!!! It's so funny that as much as he can't wait to be a thot in the summer, you thinking the same thing. Savage Szn sadly doesn't work in trying to help you figure out what you want. You have to already have your goal in mind. Step out and act on your plan. In the meantime, Mr. Convenient was going to stay in my pocket and maybe he will be seen in another book. Or maybe not, we'll cross that bridge when we get there. Lol

*Crossing the bridge

- It was just convenient…

BUSINESS AND PLEASURE

I find it interesting when an individual is able to date someone they work with. I think, (which you'll even see in my "Empire" section) it's nice to build *with* someone but when does it become too much? When and at what line are boundaries overstepped because you end up wanting to see the "Stevie J" side of things? If you can't put aside your emotions to get to the money, someone has to walk away.

Working with someone I used to date, didn't bother me because the benefits outweighed the boundaries. The number of potential connections he could bring to the table continued to multiply. I knew from the beginning I could learn skills that would enhance my own endeavors. This significant other was very strategic in the way he moved and operated. Every decision, meeting, project and assumed added responsibility seemed calculated. It took me awhile to realize those strategies were not only played out within his businesses but within in his relationships, as well.

We started off on a fast-pace, fast lane type of situation. Three months in felt like a year because we had become so comfortable with each other's company. It was quite scary to feel the chemistry and watch it grow so strong, so quickly. The open mindedness of Savage Szn made it so that I was not only unstoppable but also - unbothered by the red flags. I wasn't here for a long time, I was here for a good time. There were a few things that triggered my radar but I continued to be content in what may not have seemed to be my reality. What was real was that there was an error in our fast-track to comfort. I was not interested in watching it play out - so I left. As I say loud and proud, my cut off game is strong. I think it has been built with time and challenges that have forced me to know what I am willing to accept. When it's time to exit stage right, I grab my things...and gracefully depart.

A day turned into weeks, and not speaking became the norm. An invitation for reunification was extended, I chose not to go back into the situation. What did happen was a plan that was quite tricky to move through. How does one bold the line between work and play? Business and pleasure?

I got a call about Business. There was a discussion about new opportunities that my old *Pleasure wanted to involve me in. Building my brand and knowing that this would be a good move for my book, I saw the benefits in working with *Business. Two days later, after this opportunity to expand my territory, glory and business and it was day of my housewarming. I had a new boo coming through to show love and my roommate told me *Business had intentions of showing face. My confusion was rooted in the "pop up" part. I, personally, never do pop ups because I don't have time to surprise myself with something I didn't want to see. What I also don't do is the mixing of old pleasure and new pleasure in the same room. So what *Business didn't get from the previous conversation is that our relationship was strictly in the lines of making this money. Bringing in these coins. Bolding the line between what was and what was no longer. My business...and our pleasure. Although I don't mind his company, my house was way too intimate to be playing games with these niggas.

To be clear in case you're missing it: My old boo was going to show up at my housewarming while I was there with my new boo. So of course I had to shut that down, respectfully.

The spirit must've gave him a change of heart because he didn't show up and we're good.

The next week we had a meeting scheduled to talk about some different events that again would enhance my business. He calls, I answer. He says to meet him, I do. I was meeting up with the entire team. Let's review: What started off as a, "Can you put me on the list for your party...?" I ended up working into a quite descent move. What I was unaware of was that his new girl was also going to be working as well. In the moment I was moving in a way that aired on the side of, "I see you with your new boo, she cool". Not only is she on the same team but he literally has us with the same position and we would be working together all night. Again - this would have been fine if he did not plan to mix our business in with bringing back our pleasure. Sure enough...with the devil's help, I fell into the trap.

Of course he downplayed the other relationship with my new colleague. Although I can be threatening, I really just wanted her to know that I was *not* her competition. THAT for certain was not purpose, goal or intent. What did not sit well with me was that what it was perceived as. Even through that lens, to view that perception... niggas don't care to dissolve the mess. (How did I get involved with this Lord? Because I got out when I was supposed to and was even congratulated by one of his friends that I made a great decision.) Weeks later, his birthday came and it was honestly a great time, all uneasy feelings aside. We go back to his house for the after-party and when it's time to go home, we end up taking this spontaneous road trip out of town! (I *might* say that it was real cute! What wasn't cute is when he threw out the PSA that we were on a trip together, then to make matters more true to messiness: when I went to his house that night, my colleague who in his words "I don't fuck with like that anymore and I'm just helping her grow" was there with all of her friends, side-eyeing me like I'm the messy one. #infiniteeyerolls

Jesus fix it, I am too grown for high school games and the bad wigs. I say, "we can just be cool, let's just do business". They say, "nah, you gon be around, you're basically implying I'm your girl". (What the kicker is, is when I'm letting you know that you're delusional and tell you you're full of shit... yall they be looking at us like we got trust issues and daddy problems and just, my fav "Been messing with corny niggas too long, we don't know a real one when we see it". I. am. dead.)

Looking back, you know what? I did advise him. He didn't get any birthday **you know what from me.** He should've probably called one of his girls off his roster, because I knew they were ready... And ready, in making my own assumptions, his roster was.

I think guys get off on the drama. What I have never done and will never do is let you think that I, for any split second will let you stir up some shit that doesn't involve me getting my money!

At the end of the day, he was in this season for a reason and I see us doing extremely well in the future with the business. (You heard it here first! I'm telling y'all as I'll be relaying to him after he wakes up from that hangover, confused as to why I'll be MIA until we have some more business to handle. Stevie, stop with the shenanigans *in my Joseline voice.) Pray for me, as I pray for him. #FriendZone

IT'S AN ECLIPSE

"KILL YOURSELF! (Drops Mic, Exit Stage Left)" … oh don't you worry my dramatic breakups, you will be gone but never forgotten! Lmao, who can't forget how you played yaself? Don't ever play yaself!

So when we say it's a full moon, it means strange things are happening. For Savage Szn, strange things happen everyday. It's one thing to take an L but when the whole squad is taking L's….it's a full moon! Na, this not even a full moon, it's an ECLIPSE! An eclipse because this is just a tad bit, out of the ordinary. How do you handle a guy who just loves you way too much? When I say too much…. like I called you here to pour out some attention and you talking about you can't do this because you still love me?!?

Now, I know guys are about to go there:

"This y'all problem, y'all want a guy to love you and then when he does, you irritated. You talking about he love you too much!"

First of all, let's be clear bro, your current circumstances no longer qualify you to be in a position of "potential". I regret to inform you, you've been let go due to downsizing or whatever. What do I mean by circumstances? You had a baby… you're no longer qualified! You currently live with your baby mama… APPLICATION HAS BEEN DENIED! We are no longer on the same page financially, mentally or emotionally. In short - YOU ARE NO LONGER A CANDIDATE!

*****A nice rebound had been invited over to take you out of your frustrations, the agony of your boyfriend saying he doesn't love you anymore...the Hell?! What does that even mean. That called for a Rebound!

Lets cope with this the best way I know how. You invite your ex over and he's with the shits. Like paying the attention you need, rubbing your back because you look stressed then BOOM! He says he can't do this because he loves you too much. He can't just be here for you and not be able to fully be with you...give me a break! He was kindly escorted off the premises.

But what is the gem in this.

When I want to keep it casual, y'all in your feelings. When I want to be a friend, y'all tryna stay after for the cuddle. Ain't no cuddling in Savage SZN!! I think guys think that girls can't handle the relationship without the emotions but find the right girl in the right moment, you been praying for a FRIEND WITH BENEFITS, and you're about to miss it because your stuck in your feelings. As much as women are told that they are confused and too emotional, is it really a gender thing? Eh, Nice for What!?

THE PAST

The day before Valentine's Day I got a text message from a certain someone. I cannot be the only one who this happens to. Even when you're over your exes, those damn emotions just navigate their way into your fingers and you text back! There have been plenty of times when I have not responded but it's always that friendship we once had trying to outweigh that weak ass relationship. Oh Boy!

I sometimes think the universe does things to be funny because it knows I'm writing a book. First of all just know, if we used to talk and you pop back up, you're going to get screenshotted and sent to one of the group chats because we just know this is about to be some f*** boy conversation in my inbox. I just know. We all know. Hell, even YOU know!

Background: We were in college, I was in love… *me in love?... I know smh. (At this point my friends are narrowing it down on their fingers as to which guy I was talking about because trust - it was not a thing for me).

We lived on two different sides of the country, and I couldn't deal with a compulsive liar so eventually the situation died.

The conversation started off great and it then it ended with:

Him: "Don't have too much of a wall up though…that's how you scare away the people that's supposed to stay."

Me: "Even with the wall they don't go away though lol this guy I was dating in October called me on New Year's Eve confessing his love. I hope that was not his New Year's resolution because he needed to throw that whole list away if that topped the list. I think I was open just because I love the feeling of being in love so I'm not closed just a lot more observant of the dating stage. I wasn't moving anybody in the relationship stage that didn't need to be there."

Him: "That's understandable... You just have that type of personality that brings people close to you and that comes with the good and the bad... it's up to you to filter them out. But don't settle... you are worth much more."

Him: "Before I got to sleep just know I miss you at times."

Me: "It took me a long time to let you go and I know although it seemed like it at times, I wasn't the only one feeling the way I felt. With that just make sure you don't f*** this up because you have a family now and that's way too much to lose." (And he hearts it).

Now we're not going to bash him but let me be REAL... HOW IS THIS EVEN OK THAT YOU ARE TEXTING ME?!? The old me would've been like mmm I don't care about his soon to be wife let's FT. But you done proposed meaning that you're about to bring God into this. Nope! I have too much on my next prayer list to be playing with that fire. How would you feel if she was texting her ex? *My ex caught mine in my DM's and almost had a stroke...! THERE IS A DIFFERENCE FROM WHEN YOU'RE MY BOYFRIEND AND YOU'RE ABOUT TO BE MY HUSBAND because now somebody is going to have to die for this unnecessary stress you tryna throw in my life.

This is how the conversation went with one of my best girlfriends who is married with two kids after that screenshot got sent over lmao:

Her: "That better not be ...."

Me: "Girl yes (dead emoji). He damn near married with kids"

Her: "Lmfaooooooo. He gotta quit. What he want?"

Me: "Like he's engaged. I'm confused (confused emoji)."

Her: "Piece of crap. Trifling."

Me: "Af!!! Can you imagine your husband texting his ex while y'all was engaged and just had a baby (whining emoji)"?

Her: "He'd be dead." (Emphasized by me)

See I told y'all, we are at a consensus with the dead aspect. Most of my life, I've been the friend who, "thinks like a nigga" way before that book. But it wasn't even that, I just peep things that I know is not right and I can't imagine ruining my life with the foolishness. I watch the signs early because when I'm in, I am ALL in. I don't go into a relationship with trust issues because we won't even make it to that point. I understand toxic - when I see it. Savage Szn has just been the time period when I am voicing it out loud. DID YOU NOT SEE THAT HE WAS A LIAR WHEN HE HAD ON THAT HAT AND THEN HE TOOK IT OFF?!? #Catfish

Jesus grant me transparency over my life because I need to know what I am setting myself up for before I get too deep in.

I expect my exes to float back though because I have always been an amazing person. A relationship with me is like that forever thing and if you are not ready for that then you just weren't ready at the time. Which is fine, no pressure! I am also very aware of the upgrades that I continuously push to make in my life and I AM IN MY PRIME! My new boos have to figure out if they like the things that are negative about me or not. The old ones already figured out it wasn't something that actually mattered and they could tolerate it. Which is evidence for why they never strayed that far away.

As I come to the end of the dating portion, I had to write a snippet for Mr. Biggs. I love Sex in the City and I have literally self-proclaimed the title of the "Black Carrie Bradshaw." What I do know is, with every Carrie Bradshaw you have your Mr. Biggs. But no matter how much time and energy you have invested in a

man, he may not be there for the end of the movie, and that's okay. (Mess
around and switch characters #Samantha)

MY FAVORITE FLOWERS ARE DAISY'S

I'm immune to this heartbreak because my heart wasn't done healing from the last. Didn't necessarily rip the band aid off but more like *no* effect.

Standing in the liquor store begins the night of something like a LITuation. This was something that would leave an unforgettable mark in my life.

My mom called and she says, "Am I sitting down?" Oh God, that's our family's way of breaking the news. (My sister asked my mom the same thing when she told her me and my ex had broken up). What came out of her mouth was something unimaginable. My Aunt Daisy died in a car accident.

Excuse Me.

Who?

When she told me, I was just in shock because I couldn't imagine that this could even happen. I am here trying to let go and get over a nigga and the universe says, "F you, take this!" But that's not what God said. God said, "Don't mourn over people who were there for the "good" times because you still have people who are here for the good and the bad, and forever."

My uncle was driving the car with my aunt's husband in the front seat. Long summer drives in the south are common through the thundering woods of South Carolina. I had driven on that same road so many times. Every July 4th, my mom's side would have their family reunion - It's been a minute, but this would be a year of remembrance. There was a semi-truck at the end of the hill. As they would see it late, and began to swerve, screams of life couldn't save her and screams of a call home would take an angel away from us. Their car didn't get hit by the truck. Aunt Daisy didn't get hit either and she didn't go away in pain with bruises or scars. According to my undiagnosed autopsy, my mom and I agreed it was a heart attack.

The heart is a precious organ - it can determine life and death, in between it is the keeper of love.

My aunt was not only my aunt, not only my Godmother but she was the person my mother went to when she didn't have the answers. That summer had taken a shift in my mission. **I wanted to focus on being a savage in love but I now want to become a savage in life.** I mean the idea of conquering, not letting life defeat me... I stand firm on snatching my success, unapologetically. I stand firm on knocking down doors that will shut in my face. I stand firm in the memory of my Aunt Daisy, a breast cancer survivor. In her memory, I can no longer walk into the light but I'm soaring above it all.

I dedicated my summer way too much to an ex who doesn't deserve me whatsoever, and in this transition of focal points I could clearly see what was important: my BUSINESSES, my ACHIEVEMENTS, and my FAITH (FAYTHE). **I was the new reason, purpose, and DRIVE behind SAVAGE SZN. UNAPOLOGETICALLY SELFISH!**

I LOVE YOU MY DEAR AUNT. I LOVE WHO YOU WERE TO MY MOTHER AND WHAT YOU REPRESENTED TO ALL OF US! IRREPLACEABLE. EVEN THOUGH YOU ARE NOT HERE PHYSICALLY, YOU WERE HERE! YOUR LIFE WAS A TRUE DEFINITION OF SAVAGE SZN #GOALS

IN THREE'S

The morning started off typical, I was late to my morning meeting. I woke up early but then stalled in a decision between wearing my pink dress or my navy pants with a turquoise top. I decide on the pants because it looked like it was going to rain. After breakfast, I went to the bottom of the building we held classes in to find the vending machines. I was so thirsty from the night before and I was craving some water. Some of my students were already down there and of course the machine is broken. Since I had to climb three flights of stairs, I decided to take the elevator up that day. Don't judge my laziness!

I stepped off the elevator, looking at my students walking into our class down the hall. 15 steps towards my classroom and SLIP! I slip on a spill on the floor. My students hear it and immediately run out! I'm thinking … "who spilled this water and didn't clean it up?!" My students looked panicked because it wasn't water. They tell me to hurry up and get up…it was vomit. Yup, I was laying in some kid's vomit infused with this morning's French toast and eggs (I hate eggs). I immediately jump off the floor and try to think quickly. We were leaving campus in a few short minutes…like what the hell?!?! My coworker runs out of her classroom, extremely apologetic because it was her student who did it. She said she had been standing outside and just happened to go back in to take attendance. She had called maintenance but they hadn't arrived yet. Either way I had fallen in vomit and I just took it for what it was and headed back to my room to change.

I knew I wouldn't have time to take a shower, so thank God I chose to wear the pants. The plan was to run in, wash my hands, rinse off my shoes, put my dirty clothes in a bag, and put on the dress I was going to wear in the first place. On my way to execute this master plan, I pass by my supervisor. I tell her what had occurred and she started chuckling as if she wasn't expecting me to slap her while asking, "WHAT'S SO FUNNY!" I would expect you to laugh if you were my friend but you're not, you're my boss and at that moment I need you to act your position. Not your age. I was so pissed!

I went in and changed my clothes. Looked in the mirror and was reminded of how I had beat my face that morning. "Girl, you're still fine af!" And that's how I overcame the BS. As I'm walking back to my class, I walk past my supervisor, giving her an eye roll and a hair flip. People underestimate the power of a hair flip. I keeps me some bundles in my suitcase, in case somebody tries me and I have to hit them with that 18 inches of, "don't try it". One hair flip essentially means (to me at least) I AM UNBOTHERED BECAUSE YOU ARE BENEATH ME! I AM THE QUEEN AND YOU, AS THE ANIMAL KEEPER SHOULD KNOW WHEN TO STAY IN THE ANIMAL KEEPER'S PLACE!

Meeting up with my students, I couldn't stay annoyed because they never let me. Their happy faces and vibes are freakin' contagious! We head to the United Nations. We get into one of the UN conference rooms and everyone is taking their seats. I walk up the stairs and realize I needed to go to the bathroom. As I proceed to walk back down the stairs.... DROP! (Y'all remember the "*insert name* takes a tumble!) That's exactly what happened! In front of 300+ students and staff I fell down the stairs! I just sat there and laughed because I knew this one was just crazy! As if I were in high school, I silently scooted to the seat so those who weren't looking at least had a chance of sparing me my dignity. My coworker came over to me and said, "Just sit down!" LMAO

I texted my roommate like you said bad things happen in threes......girl this makes 4 and 5. **Crying emoji!!!**

The rest of the day - I tried to chill and not damn near kill myself. Eventually I was back to just trying to enjoy my normal day. And then I get back on campus...

Let's just say, it was event #7 of my summer in DC that had me questioning life. The good thing is the immunity level I am developing. Bad things happen and it's like I don't feel them anymore. I feel them at first, but I can feel myself becoming stronger day by day. #Growth

Finances

And when you're making more, you are more conscious of what you are doing with your money. I don't know if the word responsible is the way I need to describe this process but let's just say I spend a lot more time with my money. I wanted more and I got more. I got my first credit card and realized how late in the game I was. Blaming my parents for that one but - hey I finally understand how I can buy something real quick and pay it off that next check and your credit score raises like 30 points!!! Now that's a good. Doing my taxes was liberating but dumb at the same time, I needed an accountant. Specifically for people who are living out that entrepreneur life. That boss life doesn't make sense when you are messing up on your 1099's. #SaveThemReciepts

The final big girl move was buying my second car. Buying my first car was cool- it made me feel like I could run the world, because I had the key but my mom did most of the work. This time I was on my own! Nobody told me buying a car consisted of an excessive amount of stress - I was so exhausted from it all! #GetPreApprovedFirst! Writing down that you want more money and watching it come... I don't think it dictates whom we are but the shoes and bags that manifest with that increase... Father control my pockets lol make sure you pray for your sense of financial management with those multiple incomes.

The older I get the more expensive I become.

TAXES

Why the hell did I do my taxes by myself!?!?

If I learned anything about money this year it was definitely to NOT file my own taxes. Pass up every TurboTax offer and leave the business of the IRS to someone who collects their paycheck from handling all things tax season. When you have forms from your 9-5, that's fine but when you are a business owner.... just go pay for somebody to do it. Someone reading this narrative can attest to having all A's in their accounting classes, they may even go as far as to say they are competent on the financial end. But me, I, her, she...Faythe Ayanna Missick... I just knew I was going to jail!

Not that I even did anything illegal, I was ignorant to what I was doing and entering in what I *thought* was right and when my refund numbers showed up... OKAY! But I got that gut feeling, that something was not right. I'm also categorized as that person that has fears of going to jail...too many crime TV shows and their influence. I am also one of the most honest and genuine people you will ever meet but I always feel like I'm going to be in some crazy situation where they are just going to lock me up. Here today, locked up tomorrow. Have you seen me?! If I get thrown in the penitentiary, there's no hope. I'm just going to have to become somebody's lover until my time is up so I have a little protection. (Savage not a criminal!)

So I'll explain why I did them myself. Why I thought for a split second I was a tax accountant. My sister, who has already been made aware I'm placing the blame on her, gave me this lecture about independence. She's the finance one in the house, along with my mom but she's really on top of her taxes and everything dealing with being financially savvy. Me, the baby in the family, and her little sister...I am always asking for her help. Which is how the hierarchy functions. I don't see anything wrong with it, honestly - you were born to help me. As the older sister, by nature, that is your job - I'm the princess and she's the princess' royal helper! (Lmao let me chill before she cuts me off for real!)

Proudly, by this point I had outgrown asking my sister for help specifically so I could avoid the "independence" lectures. I think I had just decided to grow up and really enjoyed doing things on my own. But *this* situation was probably the worst advice she'd ever given me as my older sister.

While employed at the Autistic school, I was also tutoring on the side. It was literally more than a side hustle because I was working so many hours, it was like I had two 9-5's. **Let's just thank God that I can have one 9-5 that supports my living, and any other stream of income supports my additional expenses.** That experience taught me that I never want or need to feel like I need two jobs that consume so much of my time. I couldn't even work on my real dreams and aspirations because my time was consumed with Kindergarten Sight words and High School Geography... the money wasn't starting to feel worth it.

I was working in the west suburbs and it literally took me an hour to drive to the houses I was tutoring at. Some took an hour and a half, staying for about 3 hours. I was really on the hustle train at the time and didn't even realize that I was working hard and not working smart (shout out to Chinenye)! The amount of time I was consuming, the wear and tear that I was putting on my car, it wasn't worth it. Anyway, so when tax season came around, I had to file as an independent contractor and best believe I was filing my deductibles with that as well.

Long story short, a letter comes in the mail saying they need more information to verify my tax deductibles for my state taxes. I don't know if y'all have ever gotten this letter before but I just knew, I'm going to jail! They done caught me doing some fraud and I'm going to jail! In all honesty, everything I put down was right but because they sent me something back that was not my money, I start looking up how much time do you have to do for tax fraud.

The amount of stress that I put on myself, in that next 24 hours, could've just been avoided if I had the right advice. The right advice, meaning letting a professional, that I trusted, help me do my taxes. As an American, it's two things I don't play with Illinois state about: getting a boot on my car from unpaid tickets, and these damn tax refunds. Because let's be very real and transparent, the federal money I got, even if I had to give it back, that was my down payment on my new car! **People who aren't good with money: Spending money they don't have! That's how you end up in jail! Don't you get caught up in your credit and you don't have that cash!**

The overwhelming ownership that came over my rush of independence when that refund came into my account was dope. On the flip side of the money coin, I was about to be on Cell Block #SavageSznGoneWrong. I, the new sensei, showed my sister who quickly became my apprentice as she tells me to read the fine print. The tiny words at the bottom stated you don't have to respond to this tax letter. (But something told me to stop taking her advice at this point because she's the reason I'm in this mess in the first place.)

With a mind still set in confusion, I head into work the next day and ask my coworker who filed a 1099 as well if she could help me get closer to a solution. Solution, yes she had one. She explained that she gets the letter every year and that as a business owner you have to send in *something*. To which I replied… "You mean something like receipts? Who the hell keeps their receipts?!" #Jail #FixItJesus #MamaILoveYou

My last checkpoint and call on the solution tour was one of my old friends from college. She happened to be an accountant and does taxes for a living. I tell her the same story and in my heart, soul and spirit…I knew she was going to tell me I messed up. She says the opposite. She's responded just as calm, "You good, they send that to everybody." Insert hovering…thought bubble, "What you mean I'm good?!" She begins laughing and can tell by the uncertainty painted across my face...but offers some comfort again reminding me that this is normal.

Well in all actuality, I was going through it! Even in the strongest moments of independence there will always be moments when you need help. Don't wait until you're on your last option to ask for it, either. We definitely develop that sense of pride as we get more into our entrepreneurship. Everybody wants to say, "I did this on my own!" Yes you did ...go sis! But... are you working hard or are you working smart?

So I had to amend everything. (Shout out to knowing somebody that knows somebody that knows something about taxes.) My roommate and I always laugh about who's a connect and if having a connect *really* matters. THIS time my connect guided me through everything, every step and went back to check my work. Although, I had to pay some back because of my miscalculations, I found relief in the confirmation that I was not going to jail, at least not that day... !

What is so meaningful about building something with somebody? We talk about how we want our lives to be so extravagant but I prefer to have someone to share it with. That ideal Bey and Jay... we just look and want, (except we don't want the inspirations of Lemonade or 4:44). To say "we", referring to more than one person, building not only a relationship but a movement that betters the world or even doing something that changes our mindset and lifestyles...is a declaration. Don't let us actually get it or see it happening. A million pictures are taken for IG, just to prove to who knows {rolls eyes} that you have it! {That usually ends up in a failed relationship unless your intentions are truly to inspire others and testify on your blessings.}

I remember in college how my life was changing. Academically, I knew that I was at a high in my life that I had never been in before. I was very content with my college "situationships" and had never really questioned reaching for more than what it was. Til the day came that I, Ms. Missick was accepted into graduate school. To know me, is to know that I did not have all of my marbles in my education. I thought that I would end up with a great job, just living in the moment. Nope - That ended with me having to sit out a semester, to think beyond the moment and truly grasp my future.

Slight Rant /// Back to Grad School

Getting accepted into a graduate program was like getting accepted into college for my family. Undergrad was an expectation and graduate school was exceeding the expectation.

Seriously, if you look at my pictures from graduation and the number of people that attended my undergrad vs. my graduate school graduation, trust my family made it known that they expected nothing less than a M.A. in anything. I know they are secretly plotting on a Ph.D. which I may give them to grow in my self-love and shame people when they say "She's too ratchet to be …". Dr. Missick (a name and title combination, common in my family).

So... I was sitting in my bed shuffling through my mail and I see a letter for EIU Graduate School. I had applied to two schools, NYU Global Affairs program and my alma mater. Honestly, I wanted to go to New York. Born there, I knew the amount of opportunities available would outweigh the cost in expenses. My friends were graduating or had already graduated and I genuinely wanted to be in the City that Never Sleeps. My choices in applying were also slim - I did not want to take the GRE because I knew I was going to Law School right after graduate school and wouldn't need both... (in case you're wondering, nope didn't go to Law School... lol). Following up with NYU, they told me that they would not be able to give me a final decision until my final grades were released in December. I opened Eastern's letter with a nonchalant attitude and they not only said I was accepted but that I was being offered a graduate assistantship. In a decision that my parents had a big influence on since they already stated they weren't paying for my graduate degree... I stayed at EIU.

To get to the moral of the story, I sat on the bed excited to think that someone like me the "not so smart" friend would be going to grad school. I didn't have that "significant other" to call… In the moment, I not only felt what it was like to not have someone to share this victory with but I wanted to be someone who could fill that void for someone else.

I think being a teacher allows me to fill that void for a lot of my students. A lot of them come from broken families who will not be there when they are putting in time, work, and energy. Or acknowledge the struggle when they simply get an A on one of my papers.

"I want to help others."

It was written originally on my prayer list until I realized it fell in with all of my other goals.

I thought this statement meant that I wanted to do more community service at first, but I am a professional helper. I have a shirt that says, "I wanted to change the world, so I became a teacher!"

Building empires does not have to be something selfish nor specifically with a significant other. I did not know the potential of my empire in a different area of focus until I opened my hand to one of my friends, my roommate, the other half of Savage Szn.

Specifically, as African-Americans, we have trouble creating a foundation for our children and stabilizing a legacy that can last for future generations. From experience, my parents did not have that business and financial plan laid out for me but they did teach me some great morals and a lot about sacrificing.

Opening our mind to the idea of building with each other helps our communities as well... let me preach for a second and then I'll let y'all, decide if y'all want to grab some wine and come back or knock this whole book out tonight!

Hypothetically speaking, I am a Savage. (Okay, we know, how many times am I going to say that? Oh you over it, welp you already bought the book!) So as a Savage, I have my vision. My vision includes being able to build something massive. I want this project to be something that I can build with my black man #BlackLoveMatters, or even my "White King". * Note that when one has a "white king" you should never refer to him as such because that's giving him way too much power to add to what he was already born with. It also makes Black males extremely bothered, leading to a 30 min debate in Colombia #GoodTimes...

I want to leave greatness for my children. Also conquering some of that greatness with my friends turns into another heir to manage the throne. Before you know it, we have our own black communities, overthrowing the Jews and finally running this financial world and here we have it people, I have just ended poverty and solved world peace. *No Shade to my Jewish snacks!

Everyone has been on the, "What's your purpose?" wave. What is expected of you as you live on this earth? What do you want to be remembered as? Your legacy? {Shout out to M.R.} One of the best feelings in the world was being honored as leaving a legacy on EIU's campus. I think it was worded different but that's what the award felt like. I created my own dance organization that is still there today. Between being in newspapers for my talents to being rewarded for my hard work academically into honors' societies, I know without a doubt, my name will forever mean something there because that's where I began to build my empire. Which is what we Missick's do #GoogleUs. If I google you, what will they say... this is where my Brand Team makes an appearance and promotes their package deals on Image Consulting.

#BuildWithMe #Empire

To sum it up.

What does building an empire have to do with my prayer list? "Finances". When am I going start talking about getting to this money????

Well of course, empires can bring you money but you need to first, understand the true the importance of *why* you are hoping to grow financially.

Y'all said nah or...? Alright well, listen.

I wanted to be financially stable. I've grown to realize how I want to consider myself financially stable and it comes from multiple sources of income. My family took a hard hit when my father lost his job as a Pastor at our old church. *Note to the members: Although I speak to you, I still have not forgotten and will forever side eye you as I ask the Lord to allow forgiveness in my heart...just stop speaking to me. -Thanks Management.

It was our second income that supported our house and our livelihood. We did not know how much one could depend on just one job. I grew to learn that you truly can not put all of your eggs in one basket. Even outside of income, if you only stay in one lane, how do you know that you are tapping into all of the opportunities and skills that God has bestowed upon your life? (Shout out to Etienne.)

"Build with me and I will forever share my empire with you and your family."

If all else doesn't make sense, when a guy tells you that what's his is yours... You got a check, I got a check...You got a bag, I got a bag. *The choir said rob 'em sus, it's Savage Szn!

MANAGING MY COINS

Now when I said I wanted to be financially stable, I still couldn't just be out here ballin on this budget that was in my head, which exceeded my paycheck. BUT because I have favor and my father holds the wealth in its hands...Hallelujah *praise break!

Unfortunately, it doesn't work like that - all the time. The more I try to get with this financial stability before I save anything I ask a million questions. I am the type to put $100 in my penny bank and next week when I want to buy a new pair of shoes, I'm like aw yea I got it. No, you do not have it because it is only $20 in your checking account and you don't get paid until next week. But that's what you call saving without a purpose. I have many different routes that I have inquired from my list of what I call the "amazing savers". And let me tell you how it's going! I am excited to announce that I have not saved a thing but have only increased my expenses by moving into a new apartment because I know I'm about to get a raise in a few weeks. Why do we do this to ourselves?! I mean I have faith that the Lord will make a way but we feel like because we have more we should spend more! It is time to not only invest in other things but also in ourselves. I still haven't figured out the "pay yourself" when you get paid, because I am "Savings 101". What I am going to do with this increase is invest in myself, and my passion, which is also my business. When I profit from my business, i'll put it back into my business. Where I messed up on Book #1 because I am on Book #2, in case we needed a reminder... I did not invest in my brand. It's fine and I'm good because we have to make mistakes in order to learn from them.

It's funny because one of the things I had on my prayer list was to have my own business. Why did I think my book was not a business, I have no idea! It took me all the way up until I had to file taxes on it that not only did I have a business but I had developed skills that opened doors for additional opportunities such as writing a book about you and your crazy family! {This is the finances section of course I am going to throw a plug in there to create a new coin!}

I leave your pockets with this: You can make a lot of money really fast, but what will you do with it when you get it, differentiates where you sit at the table. A boss leaves old habits in the employee days section.

Career

Do we ever really know what we want to be doing for the rest of our lives? We go to school and then we pick a major for that specific occupation. You realize you suck at Calculus and you change to something that is a little easier and a better fit for you. You have your fresh-out-of-college job and then four years later you're trying to figure out whether trying to change the world was actually worth this pay grade. You realize you need more than one source of income but you don't really have the time to work another job. Then you land your dream job and even when it's time to retire you are looking at a small business you can retire off of. I don't need my career to be forever. I do need it to be wherever I am supposed to be for my season, I'm okay with it.

#TrustTheProcess

BEING THE OPPORTUNITY

Not like I wasn't one before, but this time it was official. You can't even imagine the devalue that is given to those who are "educational support". I have always been a dance teacher but it was not something I put on my resume. It was a hobby that I would throw out there at the interview when I wanted to let my interviewers know that I was cool. Teaching in DC at an educational conference where I got to have simulations on writing UN Resolutions, that sounded cool. I taught international high school students and they wanted to see my souvenirs and ask where in the world my scholars were from. Next was China, well you know how that story played out...I became an author and literally that is what takes up a 45-minute interview. China is the answer to all of the questions! What has been the hardest part in your career? What has been a bliss moment in your life? China saves me every time because I am a black woman who taught English in China. How many people do you know... lol you get my drift.

I was a self-proclaimed teacher because I was who I thought I was, until there was that piece of paper that could tell me otherwise. My teaching certification had been following me for a while. I could not decide on whether I wanted to go back to school to get certified because I *honestly* didn't want to. If I was going to go back to school, I was going to get my PhD and be Dr. Missick. And as a Dr. I would eventually be Professor. With a Master's in International/Comparative Politics, I knew I could teach community college. On the application they asked me what my teaching philosophy was and I gladly stopped answering questions. To know the technical terms, did I need all of that to teach? I had been doing just fine for the past three years in DC and abroad.

I came back from China and got my substitute teacher license. I didn't have to go back to school, I just need a B.A. and $100. I applied for a Substitute

Network and I was in! I saw this as a "Started from the Bottom...well from the Top and now I'm here." The pay was pretty bad for someone who had 2 degrees. Every day I would drive an hour to a different school so that I would not have to sit in the house and be a struggling writer. Most people do love being a sub, don't get me wrong but financially and growth-wise... I was not fulfilled. I knew it was not where I would always be and so I took the time. During that time as a substitute teacher I finished my first book. The extra minutes you have in your life that don't involve lesson planning and team meetings was not too bad. Although, I knew I would crave more eventually.

I was fortunate to land a full-time substitute position that would compensate a few dollars more and create a greater sense of stability. If you do not like an inconsistent workplace, please do not volunteer to substitute teach when you retire! You go to a new class each day and try to be their teacher; you remember back in the day when you had a sub...well if you don't I sure do!

We were in 7th period Science class, my freshman year when we almost got our sub fired. I was known for walking out of class to use the bathroom and I was a big advocate of it! This time it was my friend who had to go. The sub told her no and I encouraged along with my peers to just walk out.

"He's just a sub, he can't do anything!"

That poor man didn't know what he had signed up for. She walks out and he wouldn't let her back in. As we try to rush the door, the sub blocks it. My other classmate picks up the phone and threatens to call administration, the sub hits the phone out of his hand and it was all downhill from there!

"YOU HIT A STUDENT! WE'RE GOING TO GET YOU FIRED! YOU WON'T BE COMING BACK HERE! YOU HIT A STUDENT!"

If I'm being entirely honestly, I don't even think that man touched him. We just kept saying it so much that I think he didn't know what to believe. As teenagers...we were just being teenagers.

I actually don't know if that man got fired, decided to never return again or stayed... but I do know I got ALL of the karma. I can be 100% certain that I reaped all that I harvested in high school, ranging from getting cursed out to just blatant disrespect. I was now the sub and on the other side of the desk. When I did not think I was truly progressing as a teacher, being a sub taught me classroom management. It afforded me a practice of sorts to develop my own way of controlling a classroom, of course through trial and error but mostly through tough love. That growth from my first few times having to show those kids who was actually in charge to my last, was noticeable in my level of stress *after* teaching.

My full-time substitute positions were love though! My first position was with my babies. I was a co-teacher with Ms. O'B. She was a stern teacher and she taught me that I was the boss and if I looked like I didn't know what I was doing, they would act a fool and make sure I didn't know what I was doing. She also taught me how to leverage the power of a parent. I called grandma right up to the school when her grandson stabbed another with a pencil. She came up there and tore his behind up! She didn't take him in the bathroom, to make an example in case other little kids hadn't had a good whooping in a while. Ms. O'B not only showed me but she taught me. She was the first person to take time to teach me how to look for lesson plans and materials. We had to wing it the last two months to make sure these kids were ready for 1st Grade.

I was still applying for other teaching positions while I was working with the babies. I came across a job that I thought I really wanted. I went through both of the interview rounds and it was a teaching position at a high school. The demo was in a few weeks and I wasn't sure how or what to prepare.

I loved the school I was at! I loved the principal as well and he taught me to get everything in writing. Short and simple: I asked for a full-time position next year, he told me to apply, I applied, cancelled my demo at the other school because I knew this is where I was comfortable and waited for a response from HR. Kindergarten graduation comes around on the last day of school and I never got a response to my application. Welcome to career life! I don't know if it was because their education lead never really seemed to like me or because a teacher that was going to get fired decided to just take a demotion. Either way, I was stuck in the same position I was in, as a substitute teacher. What I didn't realize at the time was that I was on my way to being content in a position that would not be where I wanted to be. This position also wouldn't enhance my growth in my profession. I was going to end up stagnant and may have never pushed myself more.

When God has something for you, things that seem to suck in the beginning don't even matter. I applied 50+ times to positions within the Noble Network of Charter schools. I went to their career networking evening and convinced myself by the time the school year started next year I was going to be teaching with one of their schools in their network. If I could not teach, I would be working somewhere in the network. I had it declared in my mind, and with that I started making moves that aligned with this task.

Waiting on the network, I started teaching at an autistic school and my experience was something I knew I wouldn't stay in. It was definitely something I would never forget. With a social science background, getting my license would allow me to teach in Special Education as well. Here are my initial thoughts because of course when it's time to write, I write:

"And the work begins!

"I started my new job today as a paraprofessional. A paraprofessional, for those of you who do not know are the people who are assigned specifically to children with behavior or learning disabilities in classrooms. I am loving my journey throughout the education sector. From a lead teacher to a substitute and now a paraprofessional, yes, the next step is to become a certified teacher (more pay, and more of the educational background and foundation). If you know me, you know I have dipped and dabbed in many different job areas and I always see what I like and what I do not. With PhD still never too far away from my goals, I see myself being able to rise through the ranks of the education world, specifically going back to my Political Science background and looking at educational policy.

But let's talk about today!

Today was my first day and it was very intimidating. My school is for students that are 10 times the level of your average IEP student. My job is to prevent crisis and create a safe haven in my environment. Our school is not your typical Behavioral Disability Clinic because we are still a school. Our mission and focus are centered on the education of students and goals that need to be set in order for our students to become more adaptable in the outside world. It was my new adopted vision to teach these students how to push through and prevail, behaviorally and academically.

Our whole day was centered on a "Safety Test". The idea of a 4'5" elementary scholar charging you does not sound too crazy because you think they are "little kids". I vividly remember during my observations before I became apart of the staff, seeing a student in their zone and it was like the Autistic Horror Movie. I was slightly afraid. Not because of the charge but because of those few moments afterwards. The days that followed the blow up and the weeks it would take to repair the relationship. I understand that this job is going to be challenging but I am not the type to turn down a challenge so with the fear comes... motivation."

I originally set out to write so that I could reflect when things got rough. To remember the feel-good situation I was in and create space for more good energy. For many of these scholars, this is the last stop in the educational system and it is specifically designed for them. I grew to understand very clearly that these people who live in very close quarters but seem so isolated were more similar than different. There was so much they had in common regardless of the differences in their personalities and reactions.

The day I knew I would leave = when I had to change a diaper and wipe the ass of a grown ass kid. Excuse my French but let me tell y'all that this job is for somebody...anybody out there but at the time it wasn't for me. I had given my best to this Autistic school and the stories that I could bring back were something that my friends and family would continue to be considered memorable.

For example....

"Martin and that fuckin dream"

So, disclaimer... before I have Autism Speaks knocking down my door. This story is not to make a mockery of the community. It couldn't be after I built the trust and cultivated the amount of respect and love I now have for that community. It is unquestionable. Only working at this school and calling this place my 9-5 home, a few months and my eyes were opened. For this my life will forever be changed.

Ok so what happened?

Around the time of MLK Day, we have that very typical lesson about who Dr. King was and what he stood for. In a class full of high functioning autistic children, we not only see the effects of having autism but also the effects of having parents who do not respect diversity. A lot of things our kids would say were usually a reflection of what they learned at school, what they picked up on TV, or what they hear in their household. One kid in particular was clearly around a lot of inappropriate language dealing with race. As a white child, the level of blatant and intentional disrespect he fueled the word "nigga" with, came from a place of anger. He was pissed off at one of his black teacher. But to be transparent, if you were white and pissed him off he might call you one too! Although - this kid's mom was Mexican he ultimately identified with his white race. This kid was extremely smart and has to be if he's able to pick up on how strong the reaction was by calling someone a nigga. The power in the word. The emotional attack the word holds. Meanwhile, out of nowhere - while one of his teacher's is getting cursed out by another peer, he stands up and yells from sea to shining sea... "I wish Martin never had that fucking dream!" Then as he points one by one to each of the black staff members that was in the room he says, "Your nigga ass wouldn't be here! And your nigga ass wouldn't be here! And your nigga ass wouldn't be here!" Mind you it was five of us at minimum in the room at the time. Crazy - but this was common. This had become an every day episode. It was extremely hard to separate the facts from the exceptions. These kids faced issues that made it difficult to deal with a rush of emotions. As a very sensitive person, I had to get tough lightning quick! I never knew that toughing preparation would follow me in the future when a kid walks in a tells you "You're a horrible teacher!"

So where did I go next?

After many applications and video interviews, my VP invited me in for what is known in the Education World as a demo lesson. Talk about intense! I had to prepare a lesson, teach it, give myself feedback, and have an interview with all members of the leadership team. To increase the capacity, the entire department also joined the pow wow. Got the job!

Every time I'm just not having a good day I reflect back on to the reasons why I chose to be a teacher and wanted to work for the school I work for. My shirt with my developing mantra, "I wanted to change the world, so I became a teacher!" To top it all off, the amount of respect I gained for my own line of teachers and everyone else who takes on this job, shot up. People don't truly understand the pressure and the stress in trying to educate a child. The fact that my students live in what we watch on the news and are able to still write a paper addressing a history that created their lifestyles. The norm of being black and brown in America. As they learn from me, I also learn from them. As I am molded by them, I can only hope they have been molded just as craftily as I have been.

I have found that what I love about being a teacher trumps what I didn't like as an employee.

I went in for a meeting and came out with a wall. It was said, "In hiring you, we took a risk."

In having your career - what people will do is make you feel as though they took a chance on you. If you're led by God like I am, I am always exactly where I am supposed to be. I have been given skills to help with the growth of your institution and you hired me because you saw that I would follow through in my purpose. The rejections; that's not what we, what I... worry about. Rejection sucks but we can't worry about things we can't control. I wait on the next situation to shake up my life. With faith this big and an even bigger God, I know that shake is going to be done with grace and I won't be shook to be broken but to manifest into something greater. I know things are bigger and unimaginable on the end of that shake.

I'm not a risk, I'm an opportunity!

The fact of the matter is: you know your worth and there is no reason that anybody else should be able to come in and tell you what you are. As mere as throwing a word in their language that will try to degrade or diminish your ability to be successful at what you do.

I'm not a risk, I'm an opportunity!

If they can't see that it's because it wasn't meant for them to see. I pray for direction constantly because I don't want to be anywhere I'm not supposed to be. Have you ever moved when God told you to wait?! You don't get too far and you usually start right back where you were at but in a worse position. Trust your skill, trust your faith.

A risk...? I am a blessing! A risk means that you are unsure of betting on me but if you sat where I sit next to God, then you wouldn't have to worry about gambling. You win without even having to play. I have favor and I am arrogant with my blessings because I need people to understand who and whose they are dealing with. Especially when they throw words in my direction that insinuate I am, "a risk".

--Lawd they almost made me curse.

In my attempt to always live my best life and with all due respect to the season I was in, I had a meeting with someone else. We discussed what I should do about the lingering feelings of the "a risk" situation, it had been a few days and it is still did not sit well with me. Every time I'd receive feedback after an observation, it felt like "well you thought I was a risk anyway so what did you expect?" That had become toxic. I couldn't have been as risky as I thought, and it was suggested I have a crucial follow up conversation about what was intended vs. what I heard.

I honestly don't know how people can sit in something that irritates them. I need clarity and I need all active parties to know how what they said or did was received. It had been a few months since the comment was made. Emotions had died down and I was able to have a very mature conversation about it to really get an understanding. **Timing** is everything, because some of y'all will try to have that follow-up the next day and you weren't ready so that followed-up with negativity, and that followed-up with you no longer having a job. Nope don't have time for that. Since it is something that is still bothering me, I have to address it for myself but in a very professional way. I am hoping that the response is something that I am looking for and if it is not, I am hoping that I make them question their own first intentions through my success as an employee.

*That word employee, see this is why I keep writing because this wouldn't even be an issue if I was the boss.

-Ok sus the meeting, what happened?

And the day of the crucial conversation was here. I figured my VP dropped some info to my boss to let them know that I was rubbed the wrong way by their feedback because a check-in was insisted through an email. Mine felt more mandatory than optional, unlike my colleagues. 5-minute countdown until I walked in the office and I wondered, would this go downhill? Would I have to look for another job the next day? You never know what type of energy is going to be a response of negative feedback or as we say at work "adjustments". How do you tell your boss that they were wrong? What I wasn't looking for was for them to say they were wrong rather a clarification of what was said. I honestly wanted good intentions for the degradation. Beating around the bush and answering questions they wanted to know what it really was and so I said it. I told them what was said and how I felt and how I still feel. I told my boss that their words did not sit well with my spirit. I was in the crucial conversation of the year!

They apologized.

With a surprise of the response, I'm sure you don't remember saying it but I appreciate the trust in that I'm not delusional or making this up. But the ownership that I take every day of my mistakes and my areas of growth was displayed in them as well, shown with vulnerability and humility.

It came with a card.

Okay now …. don't be given out cards and then you on BS the next week... *side eye* But TO BE HONEST, it was nice to mend things, MOVE ON, AND TRY AGAIN!

Can y'all imagine if I would've given into my own pressures and gave a response that would've put me on another unprofessional flight.

My school is one of the hardest places to teach at because we are constantly making different decision in different ways. I'm sure most people can argue their jobs are like that as well. It's just a part of being human and the complexity of it all. But am I going to kick a kid out that day or am I going to let him stay? Usually one of the hardest and most common decisions I have to make as a teacher. Each class has one kid that can be thrown out but questions like: How am I affecting his future with him missing this instructional time? Does the rest of my students deserve to have their class interrupted because one student can't get it together? Am I about to kick him because I am in my feelings about something that happened last period? {Can y'all send me an extra dollar to put towards my summer vacation fund because the struggle is hard teaching y'all kids. When y'all send them there knowing they act the same way they act at home…Jesus Fix It!}

WORK LIFE BALANCE

As much as this seems like a career issue, this proved to be very much a dance issue for me. Whoever said something along the lines of doing what you love and it not feeling like you're ever truly working has to be delusional. Maybe I was doing it backwards? Trying to work and do what I love at the same time with the added stress just pissed me off to limits I was not prepared to handle.

*So, let's change the topic of this brief section.

"How to differentiate giving a f*** from well... not giving a f***."

The very free-spirited and unstructured side of me stands behind us having rules for a reason. In the same breath, there are just things I honestly don't care about. I care about the well-being of the safety of my students. I care about the safe environment of my colleagues. So, when I think to myself, when I am not giving a f*** about things is it because I am being selfish? When does the open-mindedness stop? How do you balance a mentality of viewing other people's perspective and feelings?

I think us positive thinkers (yes, I am labeling myself) like to express that we are SO positive we stray away from negative energy. When in reality, we constantly try to push our positivity on others...not by distancing ourselves from negativity but enveloping it, in its entirety. I don't think it's a conscious thing. What you give is what you will receive... but I was at a point where I was giving, giving, giving, and not receiving. I don't think I am or was sitting there idly waiting for somebody to just take on my spirit. In my opinion - that mindset of "everything is butterflies/unicorns and you get to shape your reality" is extremely individualistic. It is extremely challenging to work in an environment with kids and people in general, in a school setting with the assumption that we are all in a constant state of internal positivity. It's just too many emotions floating around, too many hormones and the job in itself is too personal.

In Dance, I wanted to exhibit caring so that the students I served and taught cared so bad that it hurts. In work, I strive for people to understand that I am trying my best and giving 110%; that shit sucks.

I always say I. am. not. ready. for. KIDS, due to the fact that I don't want to be the one to have to kill the bugs. In full truth, I don't want kids because I am no longer the one who can just sit back in reservation and cry.

(That's a whole nother situation for the feminist gods.)

I honestly don't even know what's the deal against crying.

You think because I'm crying you won't get slapped, keep waiting:

If I was a superhero, crying would be my weakness. As soon as they find out that I am a crier it's like the world is ready to get you. It's like they know what hits you. With it already seen in society as a sign of weakness, I am scared. Shook. I don't know what my parents didn't do but what I will do to my children is make sure they are nothing like me. Make sure that they never shed a tear in a sense that they are vulnerable. Never shed a tear where somebody can feel like they take advantage of the emotion. For somebody to be so vain, my weakness gets the best of me and when I tried not to show it, when I tried not to be who I couldn't be. God told me, you will die before you are somebody that you are not. My tears show my passion. My tears show my strength. My tears are a part of me and not somebody's laugh off or joke because I'm fucking emotion. I will not be the joke because I am passionate about my life. I am passionate about the people in my life and the things that I do in my life. I do not know any other way to describe it.

It's indescribable. In situations when I cry, I pray. I don't pray that God remove the emotion but I ask God to calm me down and calm things that I am passionate about down. And for those who do not understand and do not want to, just let US be.

So how I could I be invested but not too invested. I continued to put forth passion but when things fucked up, I stopped worry about things I could not control. I stopped putting my faith in people and put it in God and myself. When I changed my focal point, it was easier. #Selfish

Dance didn't care if I was selfish or emotional because dance had an agenda on its on, with "PASSION" chiseled at the top.

5-6-7-8

As a Dance coach I am extremely different from the role I play as a classroom teacher. "I'll go out there by myself!" That was my favorite line to shout into my reflection and the reflections of 16 high school girls.

BACKGROUND REAL QUICK…

I wanted to do something I was passionate about, so I went out…in true Faythe fashion and made it happen. #BGM Since I was a little girl, no older than 4, I had dreams of being in a ballet tutu, on stage as a star. This dream came true at the hands of my mother who enrolled me in ballet with the rest of my Caucasian classmates. Every year I long for some guy to sweep me off my feet and take me to see the Nutcracker! Every year I am side-eyeing my significant other for ignoring this dream of mine that will take up one of his evenings and possibly weekends. I side-eye my parents for preferring to see the "Gospel Messiah" instead of being in the magical world of pointed toes. How many years does one need to hear soloist give an Aretha Franklin ensemble on the birth of Christ? (I'll answer that. Apparently, every year this is a must.) Yet - my Christmas gift request is consistently being ignored.

From ballet I went to tap, and then to my "money maker". (No, not the strip club!) Although there have been moments when Chicago strippers remind me of myself. A tip for those who don't know: when you are in the VIP section you get a clear shot view of admiring the stallions! This is what I mean… they only send the thick girls to VIP. The rest of the earthlings have to be satisfied with crumbs shaking their "small booties matter" for a few tips. I think - NOT when it comes to spending any of my rent money on a crumb among the earthlings. I can tip myself for all of that *lack thereof*. CHICAGO STRIP CLUBS… DO BETTER! I appreciate someone who does not look like me yet can-do tricks and splits that are just magical. Majestic even. I also prefer to do the strip club the right way, in a section spending somebody else's money...HA!

So again it was not the strip club where I attribute my money maker to but to African Dance. Specifically, I learned the art of African Dance and I never put down my love for it. In middle school, I was taught this art form as well, after moving from Virginia to Chicago. I would teach my first actual class in 8th grade at one of my friend's churches on the West side of Chicago. I didn't know that my future in dance would take off as such. (Many of you reading and approaching the 100-page mark of this book may be thinking, "Girl? What future in dance?") But the idea that I was able to do something that I was passionate about throughout my life...HONEY I Lived! I dread the day my bones don't work as good as they used to and I am not able to kill the dance floor, competing with my students. (I always go against them in practice to let them know, I.STILL.GOT.IT!)

GEM...

People are so eager to marry a dream and the idea of living with how much they are being compensated. I have learned to appreciate my performances and being able to impact my students' lives the way my dance teachers impacted mine. I want them to see dance the way I see it, as EVERYTHING! You're not truly passionate about something if you can't see yourself doing it for free. (But why should you do it for free if you don't have to.) *Trust! HUNTY, I GETS MY COINS FOR THESE MOVES! I spoke it into existence that I would not teach dance for free anymore because I did not *have* to. AND EVEN WHEN THEY TRIED ME (As to why I am side-eyeing people right now) GOD CONTROLS ME POCKETS. THAT'S IT. THAT'S ALL.

I have become my arch nemesis aka the lady who rejected me from the OPRFHS Drill team in high school. I am now crushing dreams because these kids can't dance. I do try to keep it as fair as possible but I have become content in that lady's decision to cut me because I could not do my leaps. The rejected has become the rejecter. #savage, right?

Some may say this has become synonymous with my dating life. Although my data on being the rejecter is much higher than being rejected, Savage Szn has not really taken any L's. Even with the wall of expectations I've built as a fortress as a dating defense, still doesn't feel like an L. You can't necessarily take an L if you are not invested or you simply don't care. I keep this in the back of my mind, with not only dating but life as well. By not getting too attached or being unapologetically vulnerable I am not set up for disappointments. This is the pre-work for not dealing with the stress of losing a relationship, a job, money... I have already conditioned myself to remain disconnected. I was too attached to my relationship, I was too attached to my family... things that hurt me the most. When I cried outside in those high school hallways, I was too attached to my passion, dance!

Balance.

How do I remain unattached and attached at the same time? I have not figured it out yet.

It is downright offensive when someone tells you that your passion is not your passion because you're not even good at it. As we direct ourselves back to that old hag who told me I could not teach when teaching is my passion.

1. What are you doing right now?
2. Where are those people right now?

I let that shit go in one ear and out the other. If you can't give me good feedback on my shit that I bust my ass in years of research, investment, and love... THEY.ARE.NOT.GOD. #FUCKTHEM

In terms of practicing how to balance, learn who is giving you bullshit and who is giving you words for development in your craft.

GOD, I WANT TO DANCE, I NOT ONLY WANT TO DANCE BUT I WANT TO TEACH DANCE.

This year I started my first installment of my Afrobeats classes that I set up on my own. I changed my actions to make my prayers become my reality. With that came the opportunity to be the coach the dance team at my school. I changed my actions to make my prayers not only become my reality but a stepping stone for CONTINUED GROWTH.

GOD, I WANT TO DANCE. I NOT ONLY WANT TO DANCE BUT I WANT TO TEACH DANCE. I NOT ONLY WANT TO DANCE, NOT ONLY TEACH DANCE, BUT I WANT TO OWN MY OWN DANCE STUDIO SO THAT I CAN BLESS OTHERS WHO WANT TO DANCE AS MUCH AS I DO, WITH THE OPPORTUNITY.

*Like I said before, I am an opportunity and I have been blessed with the mindset of wanting to create other opportunities for others. I am not your risk…! I am your resource. I am an outlet for my students who live in fucked up neighborhoods and don't know how to express themselves. I am a resource for when my students want to tap into their joy.

How did you like your first year of teaching? It was amazing because I asked to dance more and in 2017, I did. I have no plans of sitting still.

BLACK HISTORY MONTH

Following me on Snap, you heard my broadcast about this very special warm-hearted feeling I felt on the last day of February. I would not have believed that at the beginning of the month, I would be so impacted by culture and love. In preparation for a month of particularly African Dance, I was on call to live out my passion and joy. To teach this to my students so that we could spread our culture to others at the Black History assembly. The beat of the drums, the movement, and the surprise on the faces of onlookers when I went out there and danced with my students. It is who I am, who we are as black people. We are vibrant and full of life.

It's disappointing to sit in a meeting about the black girls at my school not feeling that they belong. Being chastised for having personality and quite frankly being a reflection of the strong, independent black teachers that they encounter on a daily. This conversation was challenging to have with my white coworkers, who cannot be trained on how to teach a black student. In some respects, I felt bad for their ignorance of not knowing how to handle the small black lambs they see every day. They have signed up to be a part of a system that may one day make these attitudes and lip smacking bundles of joy the bosses and CEOs of their white children. In the words of our professors, you better network because you never know who's going to be in that room interviewing you. I say to my coworkers who are white educators, in the process of handling our black girls, be mindful of the bigger picture that they are just as an important part of our future as your white children.

In the midst of being aware and sensitive to where my black students come from, I am adamant in challenging them to be the best in and out of my class. The disrespect gets left at the door because I don't need to reprimand you with a detention that your white social workers claim is a behavior issue. Instead, I want you to understand that it's a fucked up psychological system that you will

100

fall into if you don't get your shit together. It's the system and unfortunately those who created the system, don't have our best interests at heart. *Try that shit March 1st, but while we're still in my, and OUR black history month, you're going to learn something in this class today. I am firm in them seeing a reflection of their actions and how the rest of the class who is 98% non-black sees them. It hurts my heart when a Latino student told me that I needed to get my "girl" because she was not paying attention to the readings of the Haitian Revolution. It pissed me off when my black student said he wants to learn about something with his people like the American Revolution. Don't fret, I did educate him and he learned this particular move in White American History did not free any of his people. At the time we were still considered "property". My little brother you can get more excited for the Civil War because the American Revolution is not that beneficial for "your" people. I wanted so badly for it to click in my black student's head that it is a privilege to have a black teacher that understands them. Even when the relation takes a little more work to cultivate, I as your teacher yearn to bring awareness to your lifestyle. My message is not that they have to change who they are for white America...simply be tolerant, and not be their statistic. In every lecture I gave to a black student within this month, after class, I started off the same way. "The first thing they want to say about US is that we don't know our history and we don't care about our history!" God forbid, one of them walks around with the same hoodie as that lady, "I really don't care do you?" Because as long as they see me ALL four years of their High School education, you will have no CHOICE but to fucking care! I will not let a child coming out of my class, with my name on their transcript think I am okay with them being an insult to my, our ancestors. They don't get it. I probably didn't either at their age but what I did understand, growing up in a white suburb: it is uncomfortable when a movie about racism is being played in class, and when it's time to answer questions about it, everyone looks at you. It is uncomfortable to teach about the effects of the Trans-Atlantic Slave Trade and then go in the teacher's lounge and have a casual conversation with my white coworkers like it's ALL good. Dear White people, when you see us having an attitude about pettiness that you have brought to the table, my attitude is not because I live in the past but because there are many times, that you assume that I don't have a graduate degree and my input isn't sufficient in a conversation. Even if I don't have your "certificate" that tells me whether or not I can teach. Educating and teaching are two different things. You assume that it should be difficult for me to write my "first" book during my first year of teaching, when it's actually my "second" book and I am not new to this, I actually collect a lot of my material from you. You, assume that it is okay to raise and change your tone at me as if I am a child, and when I challenge you I am a risk to the professionalism of your institution. Dear White People, you do a lot of assuming. And as much I am confused by your actions, I truly want to understand you. But as open-minded as I am, the yes girl, the make it happen, the one who will avoid the controversy because the race card is such an easy play, don't for a second think that I am not unapologetically woke. As difficult as it was being a student all those years under white teachers, it is just as hard working under the whites.

Advice?

I mean...shiitt.... Rent still has to get paid. That's what most of us do. In so many ways, I love it but DIVERSITY IS A CHALLENGE! I think I do pretty well with it, but there are still many areas of growth. You can tell by my venting session I just had, I'm still working on it. LOL.

I digress --

Outside of the dancing, the black love is one of my favorite parts. As my friends tell it, I am at the top of the list for "Hopeless Romantics". My heart dropped when I got a phone call saying that I had a delivery downstairs on Valentine's Day. My expectations now-a-days for extra-ness are a little low. (Not that I won't drop you if I see you are trying to ride on the bare minimum train, but it's easier not to expect anything out of the ordinary so you won't be looking like BooBoo the Clown with a confused look on your face because Valentine's Day done passed and you done gave all this time and energy to lil peanut head and he didn't even send you a Bitmoji with the heart. Lmao. Sad.)

I love Valentine's Day, I mean it's in Black History Month and people are just all in love and deep in their feelings. I don't care if it's a front it's just nice to not be alone in my own delusions by myself for that day. So, Shorty came through with the chocolate, Hennessy infused strawberries (It was Mr. Convenient). But how did he send them to my job like he didn't know I worked at a school.... EVERYDAY I JUST BE TRYING NOT TO GET FIRED! Can you imagine?!?

I snuck them right into the teacher's lounge, had my dance practice and snuck them right out of the building. They were delicious, me and my roommate devoured them!

Besides the love, this month brought more wealth, health, and a movie. Let me tell you why I love my people, because y'all are something else. We have spent time and energy on the Black Panther movie. We have gone to see it multiple times and even dressed up in traditional very respective garb. We are doing the sign with our fists over our chest and making sure that the world knows because we posted a picture with our friends, our families, and a selfie with markings on our face. This is all to portray our pride in what is being represented in the amazing depiction of change.

....3...2...1.... So y'all can go watch Wakanda 10 times but won't go to an Afrobeats party with me because you don't like the music. So, you can dress in your dashiki but talk about, you don't want to wear that head wrap (gele) on your head. So, Michael B. is just extra fine but you don't want to date an African because....

(Yup. I am being petty because y'all are petty for this one. I am not even speaking for my deep roots but on behalf of someone who sits with my African friends at naming ceremonies and other beautiful African traditions that y'all don't have to wait until a movie finally catches your interest. Y'all (clap) AIN'T (clap) ish (clap). Lmao. I specifically speak for my friends but if the shoe fits, you may slide your foot in there as well! *May the Social Media gods not drag me for telling the truth, and not drag me because I am not "African", I am Caribbean and let them make a movie about a magical island, I don't want to hear not one person talking about "Caribe forever". We good. LOL)

But honestly - outside of the shade, I think it's beautiful that people are embracing what we have been conditioned to think, that we have been cut off from our origins. When I started thinking about the Black History Month Assembly at my school and what my girls would perform to, I really sat down and took time to think about what I wanted to be displayed as our black culture. Let me tell you… WE HAD THAT PLACE TURNT! Started off with traditional West African dance, then some Trini Soca, then a little hip hop because I needed people to know that our culture doesn't just start here or with Wakanda but it traces back and still is living and breathing for people to enjoy! My coworker who is a member of the Divine 9 Greeks, came out and showed out! One of my students started crying and said that she wants to be her so bad. The history was so rich, and it was amazing to come and get not just our black students but everyone excited about our history and our culture! That day we danced at the school, then performed for LinkedIn's Black History Event, then I drove over to an elementary school to watch a young group of babies I taught at their dance workshop. After an extremely long day, I not only felt proud in my blackness and to be a black educator but to feel the response that my dancers felt when they felt the acceptance of doing something out of the norm and embracing their blackness, unapologetically!

That, my people is Savage Szn!

Two of my students who performed at the assembly wrote this:

PAIN AND BLOOD

Stacks of billz, Stacks of billz, I dream of havin money the size of hillz

For some reason I'm always fighting CPD, it jus seem like they cant get along with me

We fight for our rights everyday, but i know MLK tried to make a way

To all the fallen soldiers that tried to make a way, we still appreciate you until this day

I look out my window seeing my people living in the worse way

They see us living in poverty but still won't understand our pain

They don't know what we face throughout a daily basis, but still will put us through the shame

We all may not be the same, but we all can make a change

We not realizing what our civil rights leaders did for us to be here today

Killing each otha ain't the way

Black on Black

White on Black

Police Brutality on BLACKS!

What is it that we lack?

What causes one to pull his gun out the sack, Rob the sto? Slangin on the block shooting like pros?

Look at how much BLOOD we spill,

Mugs be FEENING for the kill...ANYTHING just to get that green dollar bill

I look out my window seeing my people living in the worse way

Having faith that God will send us a message, that he will lead us to a better day

Because i hear things...

I hear voices and cries of our ancestors agonizing, turning in their graves because even though we LIBERATED we ACTING like we slaves

I hear the cries of Mothers, Daughters, Fathers, and sons, families being torn apart because they losing loved ones

This pain and suffering has to STOP!

Martin Luther King Jr. said he had a dream

Well I too have a dream

I have a Dream that one day we'll live in a peaceful world and wouldn't have to worry about our loved ones being killed

Do you think today would be the day Martin Luther King Dreamed of?

- Danari Forrest

WHERE'S MY WAY OUT

I can't take it no more momma

I'm tired of living poor, tired of having to watch my back as soon as I step outside of that door

I used to dream of wearing the #24

But now reality hit me and on my hip is a 44

I'm tired of having to work this back-breaking job

And my heart has a sign that says go away but for some reason people keep twisting the knob

I can't take it no more !

Its like life has my L's on rewind

And my lil brothers only 15 but his mind sees green knowing he's tempted to join the block and live off material things

But those material things is just another dream that you had years back saying you wish you could have those things

"I'm 24 and I sleep on a couch I just cant move out

Cause paying my own bills man I know it's gon stress me out

Maybe if my father was here I would of took a better route

But I feel like a basketball coach, my whole life I was a scout"

I can't take it no more momma !

Life is really bugging me out

I'm tryna find a way out

I got a baby I can't see cause me and his moms fell out

And I'm tired of the police coming for me because I look like someone who took the wrong route.

It's like life has a gun to my head and it's waiting on me to give up

I'm so deep in this whole every time I climb I get stuck

I'm trying to stay strong momma !

But this the worst whopping I ever got

But I'm trying to stay strong momma !

Because I'm tired of my actions making you cry.

And I'm tryna live long momma but some days I don't fear to die

But ima be strong momma cause one day imma shine

- Jalen Seals

Health

Everyday - we as a society are slowly learning that we don't have to eat everything that is placed in front of you. The way we were fed growing up, we don't have to continue this in our adult lives. We owe it to ourselves to do better. To be mindful of what we put into our bodies. What goes in, always comes out.

Transparency. I don't follow these rules at all.

Lord cleanse my vagina, protect it and keep it in your safety. #DailyPrayers

OB/GYN

As usual, or as you've picked up on I am about to get real. Real to the extent of, nothing less than personal but still I preserve my areas of privacy.

"You may have HPV... ummm just kidding you don't."

Yup, shit got REAL.

But from the beginning, it started with Bacterial Vaginosis.

I was so medicated my body had become immune to the damn medication. Off an on, I would get my period, and here it came back haunting my underwear. I had to purge my entire panty collection and start all the way over.

Now before y'all start judging, let's be real. If you don't even go to the gynecologist, stop reading my book because you don't even understand the ins and outs of your own vagina. Sis, go find a doctor *now* because having a baby does not need to be your first visit. My mother was always very intentional with my sister and I making sure that we were physically ok. She made sure we understood the importance of taking care of "you" without ever suggesting condoms or birth control.

So y'all don't talk about sex in your household?...NO! Lmao.

I never realized how conservative my immediate family was until I met friends who parents were very open about sex and the effects of being involved with someone else sexually. In many ways, I wish those conversations happened because the simplest tasks of being a female would have been easier. The awkward feeling, the rush of your body being aroused for the first time because you kissed a boy. My sister and I were guessing for a long time.

I do however appreciate my mother's discreet ways. It kept a strong sense of pureness between us. Although we are now women, it allowed her to keep her little girls. And I don't mind that.

I think a lot of us want to push reality on people. For many things, I don't think it's our place. I love my friends because they let me fantasize in my delusion. It's like being on vacation, you don't bring the stress of work and struggles from home with you. My parents would take us on road trips and this now reminds me of the sweet yet small escape from our individual daily routines. I never understood why we did that, we would come back home itching for the next check to come through. We left our issues at home and for a few days, had a sense of peace. When my mind is running, the first thing I pray for is peace. I know how to get in tune with that vacation feeling in my head without even having to go anywhere. They say it's delusional, I say it's me sitting on a beach in Santorini, mental therapy

For my mom to live in a world where her girls deserve the purest form of white wedding dresses... A Reach. Yep! Lol but I don't mind giving her that.

In order to be realistic with my prayer list, I had to be realistic with the things that I thought were not an issue because I did not want to be labeled. I had BV and for a few years off and on, my gynecologist was treating it like it was just "a thing that happens to women" but how do you explain that to niggas? Thank God for this f-ed up relationship I was in at the time because I only had to explain it once. He didn't understand it because I didn't fully either. My ex was the first one who made me see how serious BV could be when he started questioning the side effects it could have on a pregnancy. This year, it was added to my prayer list and when everything else was getting crossed off, I was excited because I knew I would no longer be restricted. Then **BOOM**

"We found abnormal cells in your uterus and they may be precancerous!"

LAWD, TAKE THE WHEEL JESUS BECAUSE I'M FALLING OFF THE CLIFF AND I NEED YOU TO BE A FENCE UNDER THIS CAR!"

It was not the abnormal cells part, it was the "cancer". My Aunt Daisy survived breast cancer, and my mom survived thyroid cancer, and I did not want to play Russian Roulette with cancer in my uterus.

Background info... I usually went to the gynecologist every 6 months, more often then most because of BV. I went in March 2017 right before my 26th birthday because I knew my mom's benefits were about to be cut off, snatched from under my feet. Everything came back and my pap smear was fine. The next time I would go, would be in late fall when my new benefits from my job kicked in. Late October, I got the call after a week saying that all of my test results were fine and it would take another week for the paps results. Okay cool - that's how it normally works, they call me to tell me I don't have HIV or Herpes and then they send a letter in the mail saying my paps results are clear. My doctor called back a week later, I had just got off the train from work and I was en route to drive to drop off a report card for one of my students (dropping off a report car smh, if you know about this life then you know where I work.. lol). I answer the phone and my gynecologist tells me my abnormal cells may be precancerous. I was fine for the first five minutes after this call. Then, suddenly I just *knew* I was going to die. It is something about when someone says cancer, death is the next word that comes in your head. I didn't know how I was going to tell my family and friends that I was going to die.

I called my mom when I got myself together and she said, " Well you know we have our faith so we're not worried about anything that was said". She immediately starts looking for other doctors to get a second opinion. I continue with the regularly scheduled program, driving south to drop off the report card. I called my sister on the way back and she said the same thing, "we have our faith". I am pretty sure I should not have been driving in that moment of turmoil but I probably would've been a wreck if I went home alone by myself. I had the weekend to adjust to the news and of course the timing, I didn't have time to sit and think about it because I was taking a road trip to my alma mater for the weekend. I called my best friend over that night and she was just as bad as me. Again, you say cancer and people think death. By this time, I was not crying as much anymore, just hoping for the best, I had my faith. My biggest tears from the day my doctor called and told me, came when I thought... "I can't leave my mommy." My Aunt Daisy who passed that summer was her best friend, and I told God, "I cannot leave her like this." I was not going to leave her, when her best friend just passed. I know the love my mother has for me and who I am in her eyes, I was not going to do that to her. For someone who acknowledges my selfishness, I couldn't even think about myself in this act but the feelings of the people in my life.

I had to have a cystoscopy. My coworker at work, told me she had one back in college and honestly the fact that I knew somebody who had went through this before was comforting. She told me it happens when you have HPV and it's not as uncommon as I would think. Alright, I thought...well let's get this procedure on and let's figure out what's going to happen next. Meanwhile, my mom was still pushing for me to go to another doctor for a second opinion and I was brushing it off. She was over the fact that I had BV for so long, it just did not make sense to her. She thought that it had something to do with the abnormal cell growth. Being stubborn, I just wanted to go with whom I knew for now. I did not want to be on a grand scavenger hunt for different doctors; it was already a lot to be taking in at once. I wrote on my prayer list that I wanted to get rid of BV, not get something worse. I still had faith, and I look back and realize how strong and deep my faith ran. It was because in the back of head I knew that this situation was going to be the breaking point situation to getting rid of BV.

The day of the cystoscopy, I was extremely nervous. I went to the hospital right after and my gynecologist starts going on and on about HPV. I was so confused; I thought you said I may have cancer, what did HPV have to do with anything?

She says, abnormal cells could mean that I had HPV. ... Um hold on, I had those three shots before I went to college so I would *not* get it. She said they are just preventative shots, which does not guarantee it will not happen. After the surgery, this was another cry fest because I knew you could get rid of cancer. I have seen people who have lived with cancer, cut it out, it comes back, cut it out again, and then you get rid of it.

Who the hell you know that has gotten rid of HPV? So you telling me I may have to live with this bullshit? Nope, I wanted the cancer. Just let me die (Just kidding you, this whole book is about speaking things into existence, so let me CHILL!). Now I have to explain to men that I would potentially date that I have HPV. They don't know what BV is but they damn sure know what HPV means! Which I mean I thought I was coming out already knowing I may have cancer, not that I may have HPV. I hope I am not being over dramatic but this shit is a WHOLE mess. 2017 you have done yourself in!

The next day, life carried on and I had to go to work. My mood could be described with two adjectives: 1. Pissed and 2. On edge. It was like hearing I had cancer all over again. My coworker reminded me that the symptoms and my self-diagnosis were for HPV. She definitely told me that but I didn't hear her at the time. Since my doctor didn't say that on the phone, it just didn't register in my head that that is what it would be. I just didn't think that's what it was. I just didn't. Okay life, Okay. God, it's yours I don't have the tools, the words, or the mindset to make this mountain move. It's you're turn.

INSTANTLY.

A week later, she called me back with the results. The cells were not cancerous nor did I have HPV. The tornado that was spinning had finally stopped after a month of just guessing. I told my mom and she said great. You could hear the relief in her voice. She still had an appointment set up with another doctor; she explained that this is why we're getting a new one. I'm like ma'am, I just got great news I don't want to go through this again! If she had to drag me to that office herself, she was determined to do so. She made it clear she was not playing with my old gynecologist no more.

It was December 21st and I did not know if I was going to scratch "be healthier" off of my prayer list. Although I didn't have cancer or HPV, I had still hadn't gotten rid of BV.

I went to the new gynecologist who was young and had on a cute heel, very different from my previous gynecologist... cute! Lol. I told her my situation and she told me she actually knows my gynecologist and knows she is a good doctor as well. My new ~white doctor would be the one to cross off the last thing on my list. She told me I had BV because my body does not make enough acid for a healthy PH Balance. This doctor had me begin taking Probiotic vitamins.

January 1st was the last day of my cycle and the first day of me being free of BV. It's been six months now and my vagina is amazing. My yoni is poppin. If I had not had that HPV scare I would not have went to another gynecologist to tell me the simplest thing that could have been changed the way my last few years went.

Moms ALWAYS KNOW! - EVERY TIME

I always ask people when they talk to me about writing a book, are you ready to put yourself out there? We are all voices for somebody, and in this section of Savage SZN, you cannot expect to be your best if your body is not at its best. Eating better, living better. I am constantly looking at the choices I am making that affect my body. Having peace in your mind, going to the doctor and taking actions that are needed to be the best you by any means necessary. Be woke in ALL aspects of your life.

NEXT STEPS

On the last day of 2017, I had a slow day. I woke up in a good spirit but I could feel it moving within in me. My body was still but my spirit was saying get up and do something. I had texts on my phone from my friend Leon and my sister asking who was going to church with and what church they were going to. I waited for my sister to respond to see where she was headed and I replied that I would go there too. I hoped in the shower, not rushing but just moving at an excited pace. I don't know if I was happy that this year was over because it had so many obstacles or if I was just excited for the things that this New Year would bring. I think it was a combination of both, that relief that you made it through and I am ready for the new season. It's interesting because I felt like my life shifted before the New Year came, my New Year started early. Probably around the time the school year began. Fortunately, I did not have to wait for the New Year to come along to recognize what I wanted to change, how I was going to change it, and when things would happen. I did not have a New Year's resolution because I was not thinking specifically about what I wanted in my future. I recently began looking at my 5 year goal as a result of my 1 year goal rather just jumping into something totally new. I was missing steps in the preparation for a shift because I had never before made a plan for my life. 2017 was the first time I did that.

So I went to church on Sunday and the devil was already busy because my lyft driver's GPS sent me to another location. *Now I specifically put the right address in his app but when it translated through the phone it told me that I was supposed to be going this way. It put me in the middle of nowhere. Catch this because I don't want you all to miss this. (As Pastor Epting would say). I told him that I was going to the UIC campus but his GPS pointed him in the opposite direction that put me in the middle of nowhere. We were literally on a bridge and there was nothing there. If my driver would have had trusted what I was saying* *because I knew where I wanted him to end up and where he was supposed to go, we would have been there on time. But it's kind of like when we ask God where we need to be and how to get there but we end up trusting our own route and our own directions, on our time and we end up wasting our time and damn near missing the blessing. *Read back over it again in case you almost missed your blessing* I was trying to tell the driver where to go because I knew where to go but because he put his faith in something more familiar and convenient, I almost missed out.*

In 2018, I will trust the process, the directions, and the timing.

I get to church and I was hoping to be blessed with clarity on moving, specifically in how I needed to move this upcoming year. I feel that I am quite content not in everything but I need clarity in direction. I came out of church knowing that it is ok to be patient in your wait but I also need to trust when God has told me something and follow through. I get what I think is a message from God, start thanking God for the vision, then ask is that what I was supposed be seeing? I struggle with not just having faith in God but faith in my relationship with God. I need to work on my strength in trusting that yes, it *is* for me. The confidence and comfort in knowing that everything I have is meant for me and as surreal as it might be, there is no need to question my blessings and my favor.

I asked my coworker who is so calm yet strong-minded (people at times, don't understand how to handle it) what is it like to be 30? She said it's amazing! Because you're not worried about things you used to worry about. When you have lived through and seen that every time things work out, it's a reminder that things are going to be okay.

That last day of December was very slow motion. It was just a day full of time. I got home, ate, and had time to sneak in a nap. After the nap, I woke up and hoped in the shower to get ready for the night. When I got in the shower (my safe haven) I started thanking God for everything that happened to me in 2017, the good and the bad. I appreciated the experience and the vision of what

Savage Szn had become to me. The stamp that it made on my life and what I wanted it to do for the lives of others. It's not the first year that is going to be hard and it surely won't be the last but with so much negativity, I learned to channel my positivity and recognized when it needed to be recharged.

That night my friend, had an event and I saw a bit of behind the scenes work needed to pull of an event that hosts 600+ people. I've never seen anything come together like that, something that demanded a great amount of time and effort. I give it a 9.5/10. A half point taken off because the balloon drop didn't drop on time. But who cares?! We're so worried about that .5 that interrupts our day. I had so many .5's throughout 2017, what does it even mean to my life now? ...Nothing.

That was a very intoxicating night but the drinking - my vice, wasn't. The bitterness from what I thought I would be walking out of, turned into a mindset shift...I have a lot to be grateful for. It was never about the tears, but always about what you were going to do after they stopped... It was and will forever be, Savage Szn.

2018, A NEW LIST

1. Family

I didn't think that I would be creating a prayer list this quickly into 2018. Last year, my prayer list didn't start until June, where I had a clear direction of where I wanted to go in life. But it's funny how life has a way of moving you faster than you expected. This first prayer request is something near to my heart. It's a struggle that I have been dealing with a long time.

Growing up a Pastor's kid, you are basically church royalty. You eat first, you get the best seats in the house, if you want something done in the church for you and your friends, you just ask your dad and it happens. What people don't see is the time that is taken away from you because of the role that your parent is in. My father was not only a teacher to the people of God but a guidance counselor, the person you called on when you needed prayer, the person who takes in everyone else's emotions. The biggest thing that it took was time, his family's time, an overall sacrifice for God.

I remember on my 8th grade graduation, I was about to cross the stage and I kept looking and looking for my father because he was running late from the church. He showed up right on time! What I didn't know is that he would have to leave early to go back. I recall being so angry that I told him to not even bother coming to my graduation dinner at all just go straight to that church. That same church that voted him out because he called them out on their stealing and bullshit. We were there and people were not. I sat many days with him in our hotel room at the In-Suites when we didn't have a home because the church took away his income. Our income! Nobody gave a damn about his family or how those actions affected us.

For 18 years of my life my father was a Pastor and when he stopped in a way I saw it as a break. A break from this lifestyle of having to be the perfect

Pastor's kid and my father having to be stressed from other's people's problems. We prayed, as a family, that we would get back to our middle class lifestyle we had lived for so many years. Our prayers were answered. Our comfortability was back. After making it through cancer and repossessions, our family was back to normal except for my dad's career. Pastoring was his everything and I know how hard it must have been to have that taken away from him. I knew how much he loved it, I was just confused on whether it was his love for God or the love for the church that I would be upset with.

Daddy went down to Indiana to preach at a church and told my mom that it was just a visit. He came back from that visit stating that he had agreed to be their Pastor. "I have to go where God calls me." How could God tell you to leave your family? That's the thoughts that I had in my head. From New York to Virginia to Chicago, the work of the church has led our family, specifically my mother to just up and leave. You think about children whose parents are in the military and have chosen a lifestyle that requires them to put something else first. I wasn't ready for it to happen again.

In Chicago, it's only my mom, dad, sister, and I. So I can't say too much about my parents wanting to move, I am out of the house and on my own. But I just knew my mother would be staying and this would take affect her. Just another day, God testing my faith! Knowing my dad is willing to live apart from my mom is heartbreaking, for me.

2018, Prayer List

1. FAMILY

I wrote earlier about my Aunt Daisy and that may have been a piece of my heart but for my mother she meant A LOT to her! She's gone and my father is too. She spent 29 years of her life sleeping next to the same man, eating at the same table, loving him day end and out and that's about to be gone, for God? You watch on TV how these women live expensive and beautiful lifestyles on the expense of a sacrifice. I love my parents so much and with so much anger grasping in my veins... I would need a few nights to cry this out. I didn't know what it was like to be at my parents' house with only one of them.

A few weeks later, I took my mom out to Easter dinner and at that point I realized, a new picture was being painted in our family and my father wasn't going to be there every time. Maybe tomorrow, maybe next month, but he was not here today.

2017 was a test to get me ready for 2018, Savage Szn, it's not over.

Savage Szn, the journey still continues to be amazing and filled with chaos! If you are reading this, I say THANK YOU. And with that, I have one more story left:

Gone but Not Forgotten

My roommate comes into my room, asking was I looking for something under her bed. I said, "Nah, I've been napping. Why wassup?"

She grabs her phone and makes a call. #HerEX

"{Insert First Name} FUCKING {Insert Last Name}! You broke into my house and stole from me!"

I am weak at the fact that this special type of human being would actually steal something that requires internet, when he doesn't have internet! {But let me not call him broke because then y'all be ready to fight… he was transitioning #SmilingEmoji}

But honestly, what in ALL types of goofy! LMAO

I am also nervous af because someone was in the house without me even knowing. AW NAH SUS!

"Ayo Ash, I GOT BAIL MONEY! TIFF GO GET THE STRAP!"

… TO BE CONTINUED {SAVAGE SZN 2.0}

PEACH X POODIE, SAVAGE SZN

Made in the USA
Lexington, KY
15 February 2019